Microsoft Dynamics 365 Study Guide MB6-895

Financial Management in Microsoft Dynamics 365 for Finance and Operations

Valarie Balakrishnan

ISBN: 9781796688566

Table of Contents

BUDGETING

Budget Control Setup and Configuration

1. From Budgeting open Budgeting Parameters to setup validation and budgeting information
   1. See MS docs 'Budget control overview'

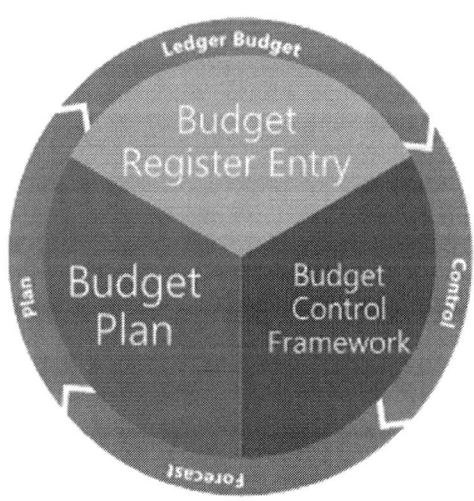

2.   Note menus under Setup

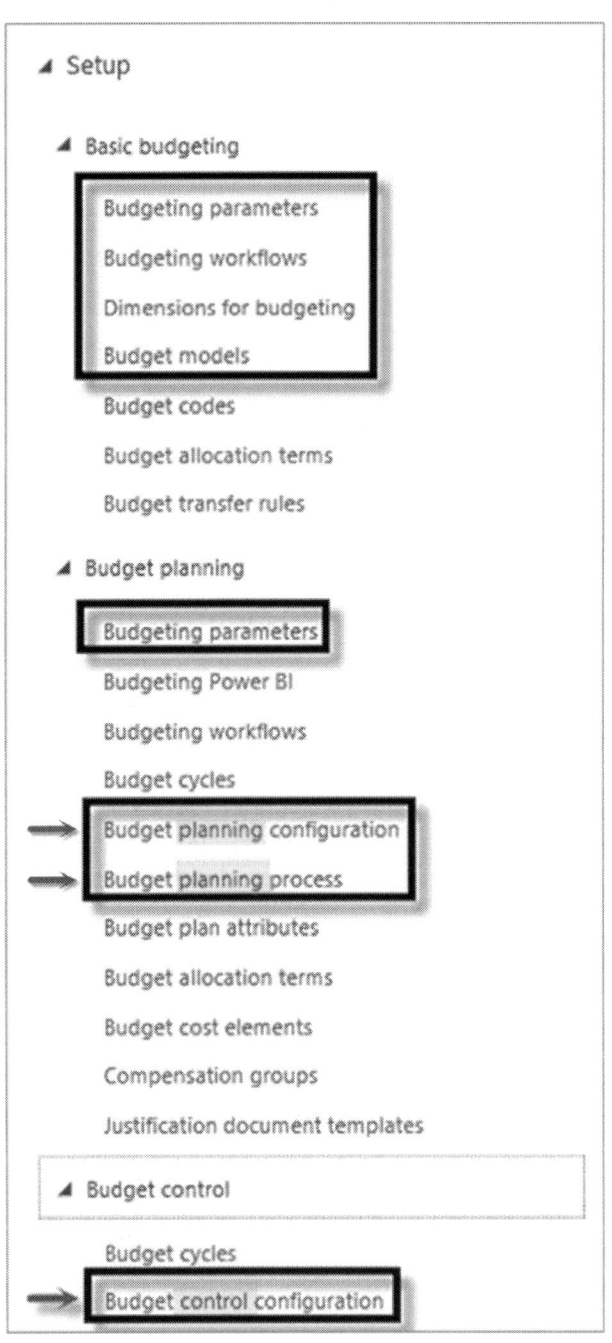

2. From Budgeting open Budget <u>Planning Configuration</u> (see MS docs: Budget planning overview)
   1. Use budget planning to manage plan configurations
      1. **Create**
      2. **Analyze**
      3. **Approve**
      4. **Finalize (Activate)**
   2. Note that budget planning concepts are represented by the fast tabs
      1. Scenarios fast tab

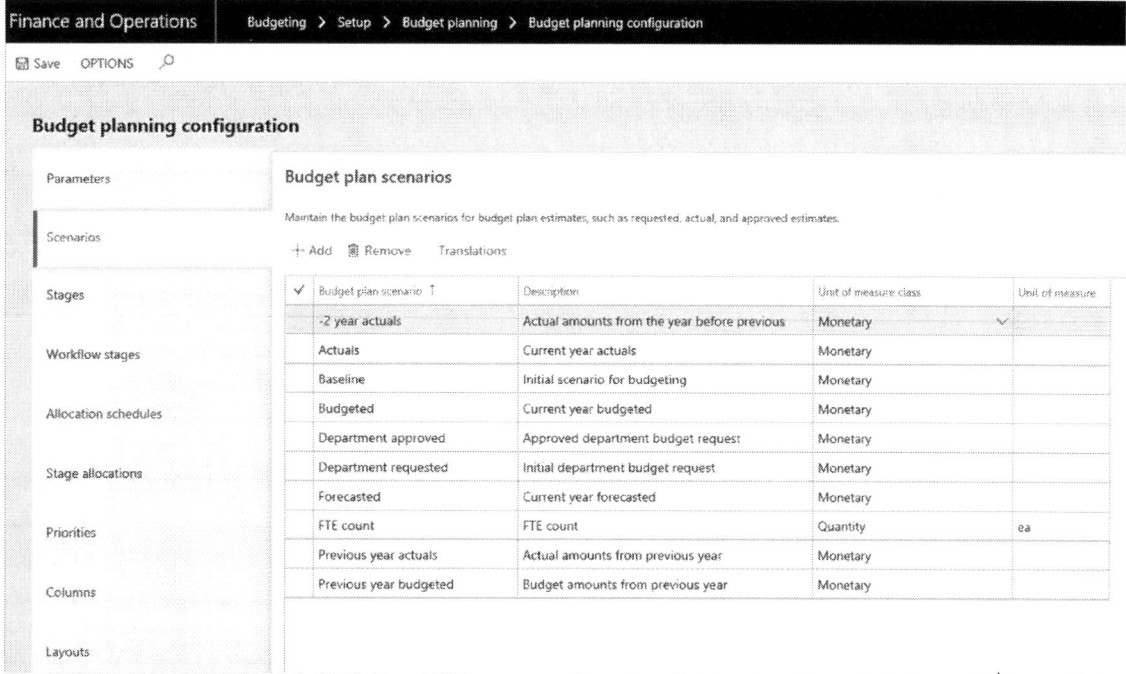

2. On Stages fast tab
   1. Defines the steps the plan follows from creation through approval

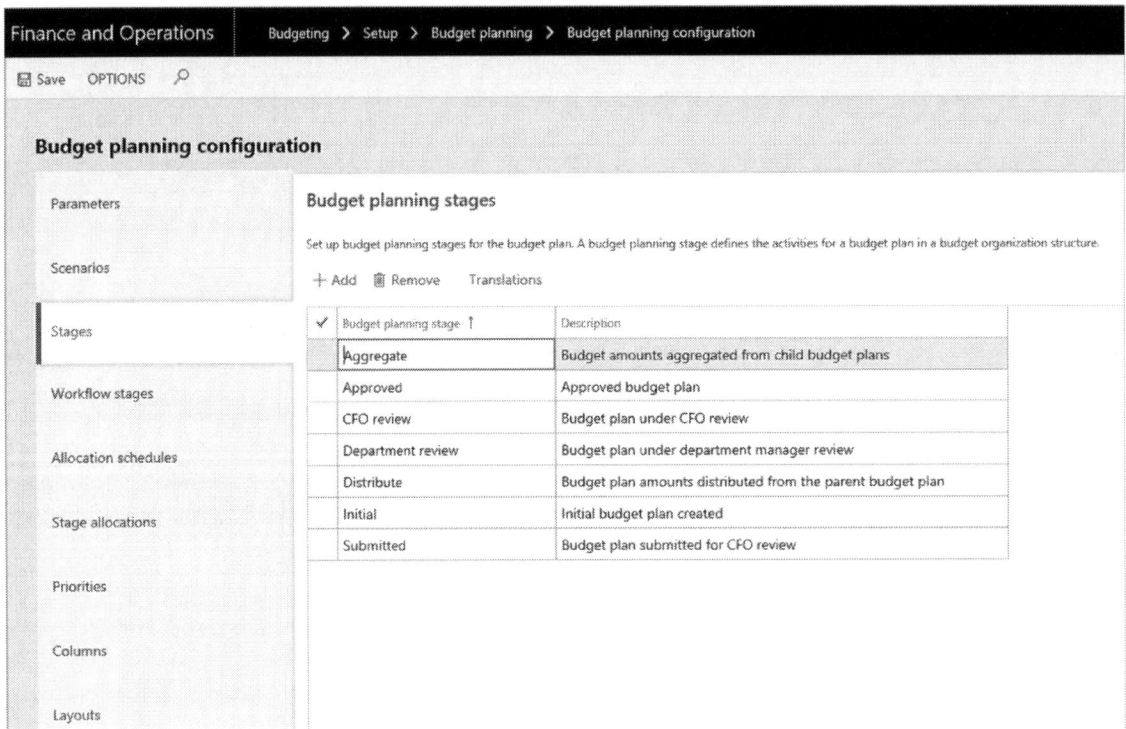

3. Workflows fast tab

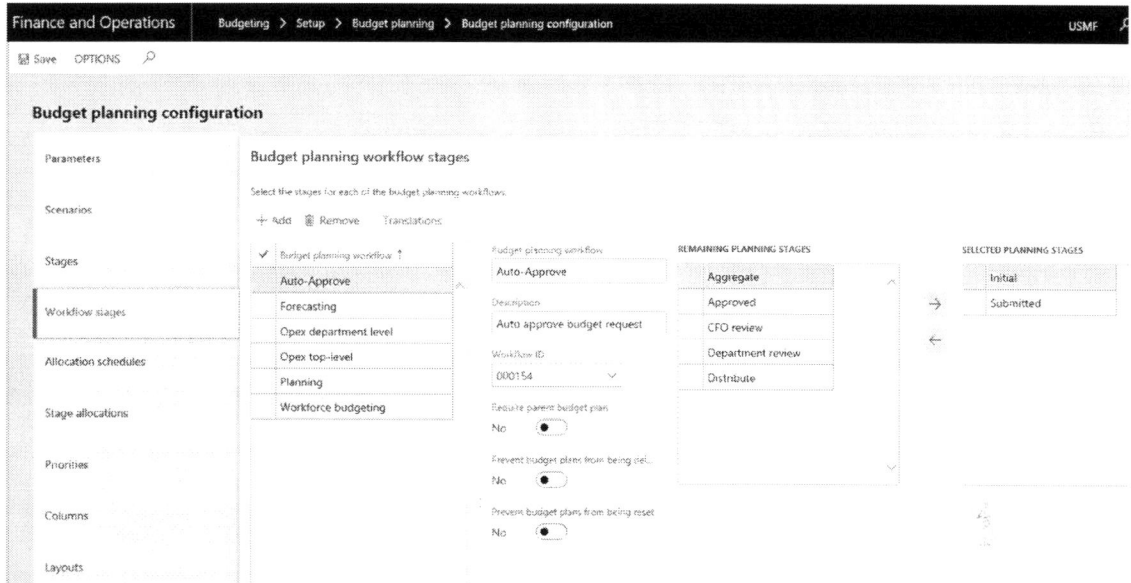

4. Allocations fast tab

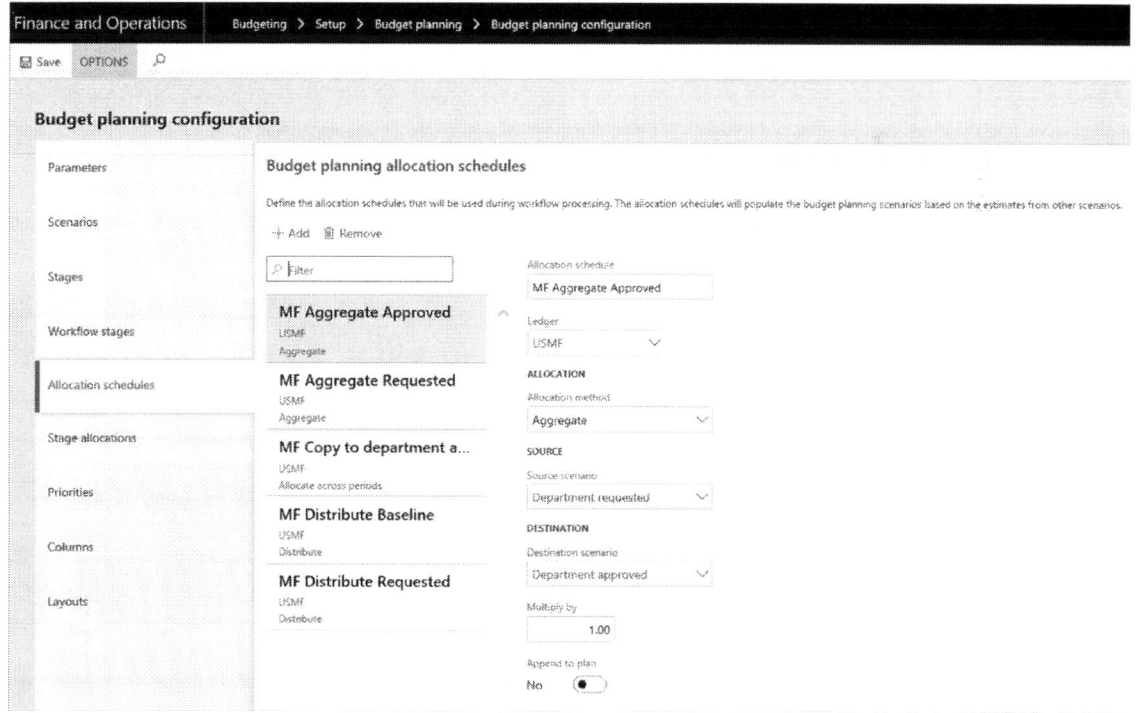

3.   From Budgeting open Budget <u>Planning Process</u>
      1.   Use this form to setup how plans are updated, routed, reviewed
            and approved in the budgeting planning organization hierarchy

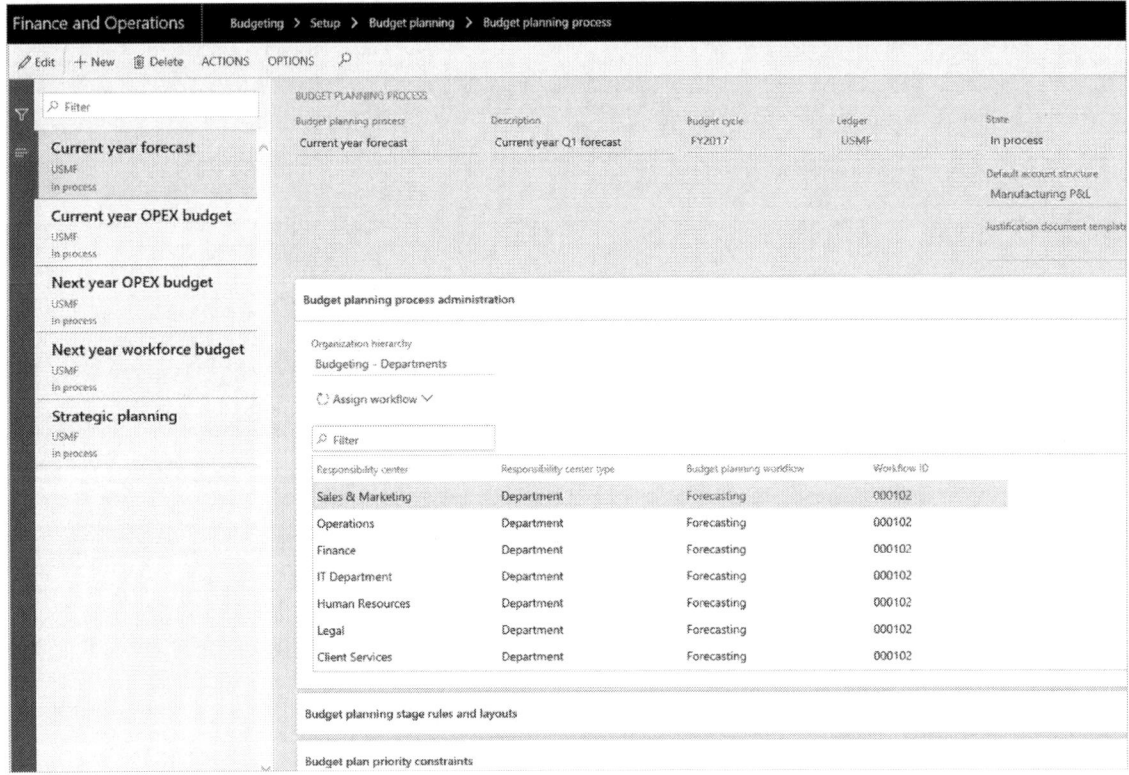

4. From Budgeting open Budget <u>Control Configuration</u> (See MS docs: 'Set up budget control')
   1. On define Parameters fast tab
      1. Select account structure
      2. Define dimensions
      3. Budget threshold is % of the budget that can be spent (can be > 100%)

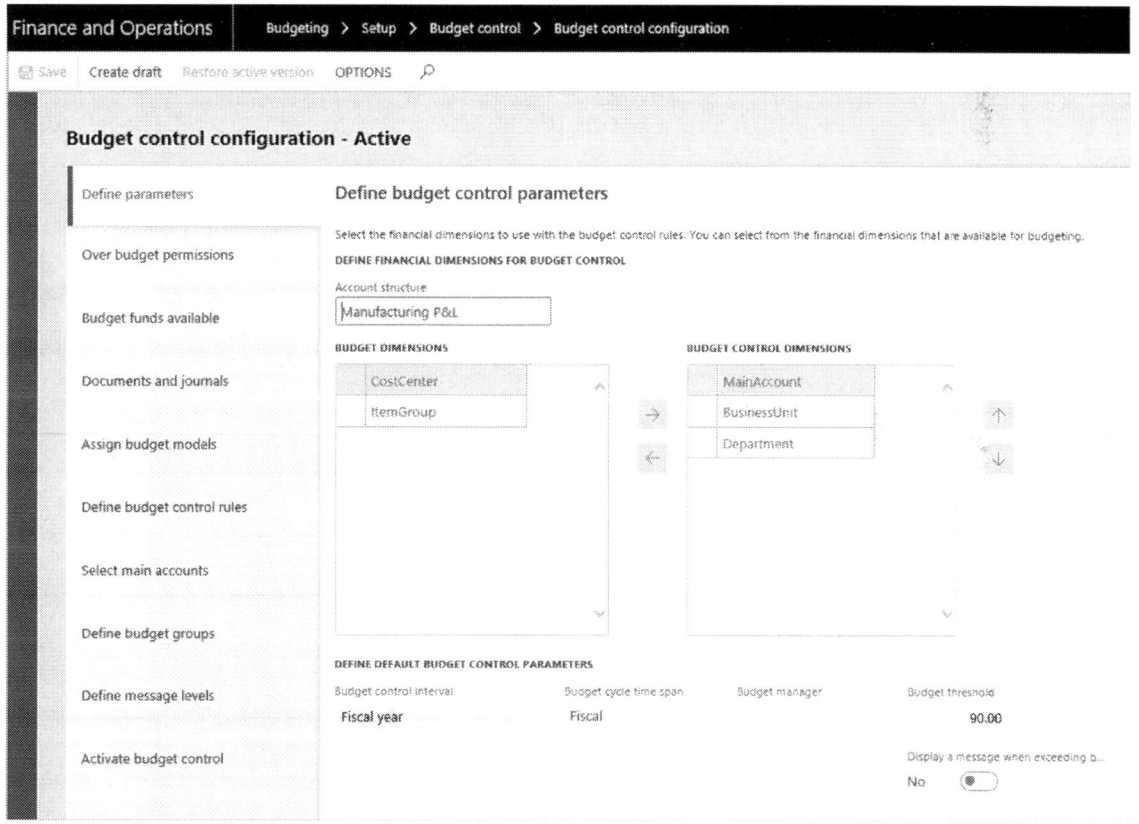

2.   On Over budget permissions for <u>user groups</u> fast tab

      1.   Setting options
           1.   Prevent over
           2.   Allow over
           3.   Prevent processing at over budget threshold
                1.   Prevent processing, applies to all users not in a user group
      2.   Use in conjunction with the define budget control rules fast tab

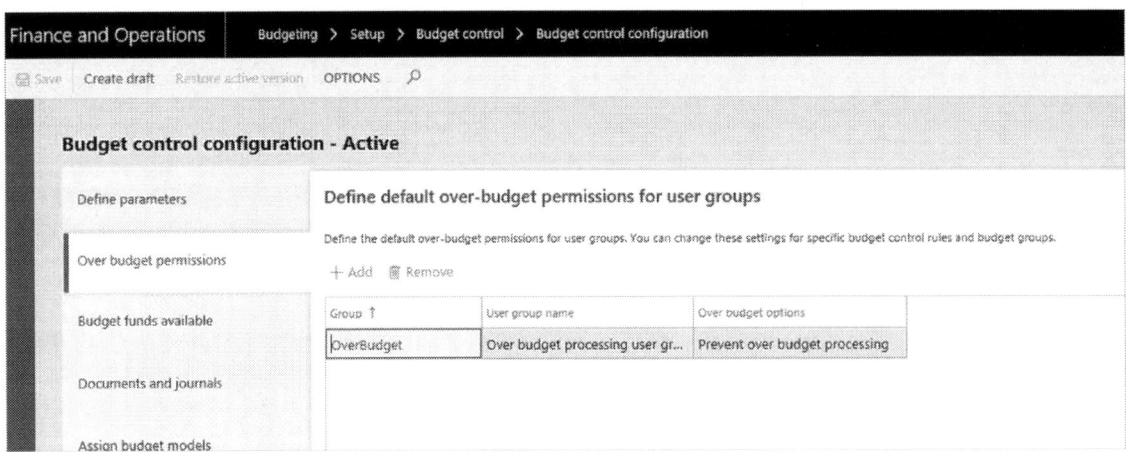

3. On Budget funds available fast tab, set funds available for planned or actual transactions
    1. Determines amounts added to or subtracted from funds available

🖫 Save   Create draft   Restore active version   OPTIONS   🔎

Budget control configuration - Active

Define parameters	**Define the calculation that determines the budget funds that are available**
Over budget permissions	Select the amounts for the calculation that determines the budget funds that are available.
Budget funds available	**AMOUNTS TO SUM** **AMOUNTS TO SUBTRACT**
Documents and journals	
Assign budget models	
Define budget control rules	
Select main accounts	
Define budget groups	
Define message levels	
Activate budget control	

AMOUNTS TO SUM

- ☑ Original budget
- ☐ Preliminary budget
- ☑ Budget revisions
- ☐ Draft budget revisions
- ☑ Budget transfers
- ☐ Draft budget transfers in
- ☐ Draft budget transfers out

AMOUNTS TO SUBTRACT

- ☑ Actual expenditures
- ☑ Unposted actual expenditures
- ☑ Budget reservations for encumbrances
- ☑ Budget reservations for unconfirmed encumbrances
- ☑ Reduction to budget reservations for unconfirmed encumbrances
- ☑ Budget reservations for pre-encumbrances
- ☑ Budget reservations for unconfirmed pre-encumbrances

CARRY-FORWARD AMOUNTS

- ☐ Include carry-forward amounts
- ☐ Maintain carry-forward status for documents

BUDGET APPORTIONMENTS

- ☐ Use only apportioned amount

Budget funds available = (Original budget + Budget revisions + Budget transfers) - (Actual expenditures + Unposted act reservations for unconfirmed encumbrances + Budget reservations for pre-encumbrances + Budget reservations for unc

4. On Documents and journals fast tab, set source documents and journals needed for budget control
   1. Best practice – match documents to budget funds available selections
   2. Journals, enables journals subject to budget control

Finance and Operations | Budgeting > Setup > Budget control > Budget control configuration

Save | Create draft | Restore active version | OPTIONS | 🔍

Budget control configuration - Active

- Define parameters
- Over budget permissions
- Budget funds available
- **Documents and journals**
- Assign budget models
- Define budget control rules
- Select main accounts
- Define budget groups
- Define message levels

Select the source documents and accounting journals for budget control

Select the source documents and accounting journals that are subject to budget control. You can also select specific document a select the corresponding Relieving documents.

Document/ journal ↑	Selected	Check at line en...
Advanced ledger entries	☐	☐
Allocation journals	☑	☐
Daily journals	☑	☐
Expense reports	☑	☐
Fixed asset journals	☑	☐
General budget reservation	☐	☐
Payroll pay statements	☑	☐
Project expense journals	☑	☐
Purchase orders	☑	☐
Purchase requisitions	☑	☐
Travel requisitions	☑	☐
Vendor invoices	☑	☐

5.   On Assign budget models fast tab
    1.   Budget models perform budget checking during the budget cycle

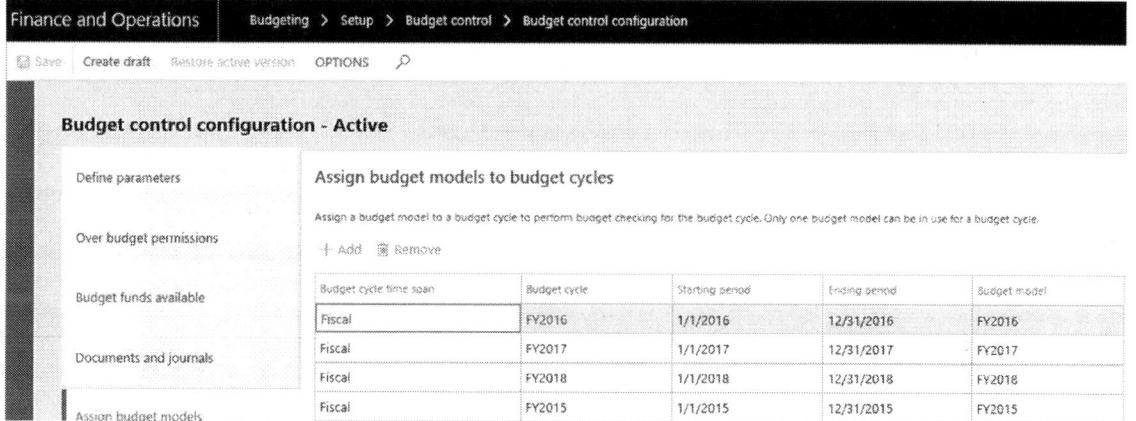

6. On Define budget control rules fast tab
   1. Rules are <u>required</u> for budget control
   2. Define for combinations of departments and cost centers based on dimension value combinations

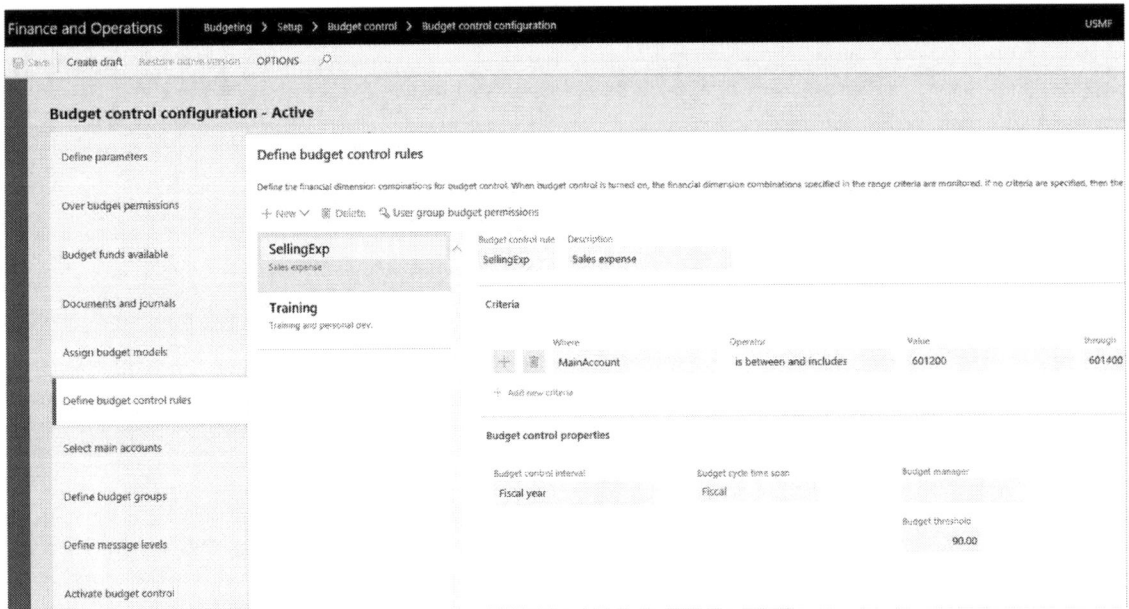

7.   On Select main Accounts fast tab
     1.   Used if the main account financial dimension is not used
     2.   Selects accounts the budget control rules will be enforced for

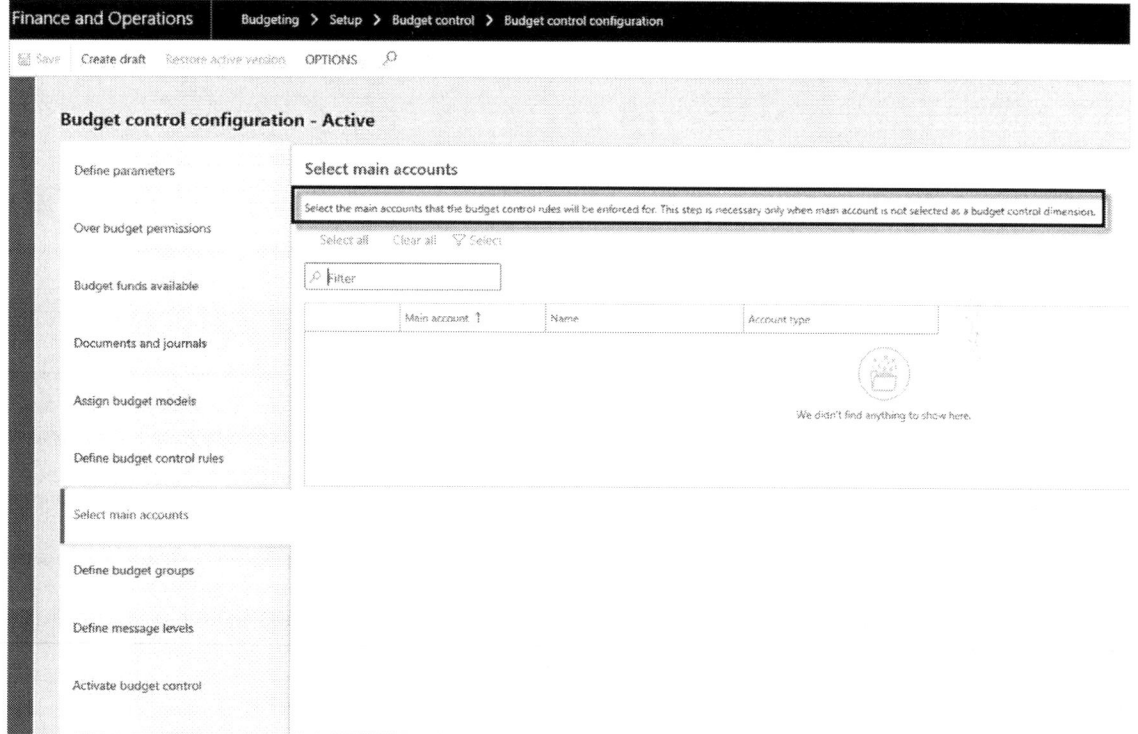

8.   Define budget groups fast tab (optional)
9.   Define message levels fast tab (optional)
10.   On Activate budget control fast tab, activate

Create Budget Plan

1.　　From Budgeting open Budget Plans
　　1.　　Enter
　　　　1.　　Process (mandatory)
　　　　2.　　Center
　　　　3.　　Parent Plan (if applicable)
　　　　4.　　User Group (if applicable)
　　　　5.　　Currency
　　　　6.　　Plan Name
　　　　7.　　Priority
　　　　　　1.　　Priorities are setup during plan configuration and the priority is selected when the plan is created

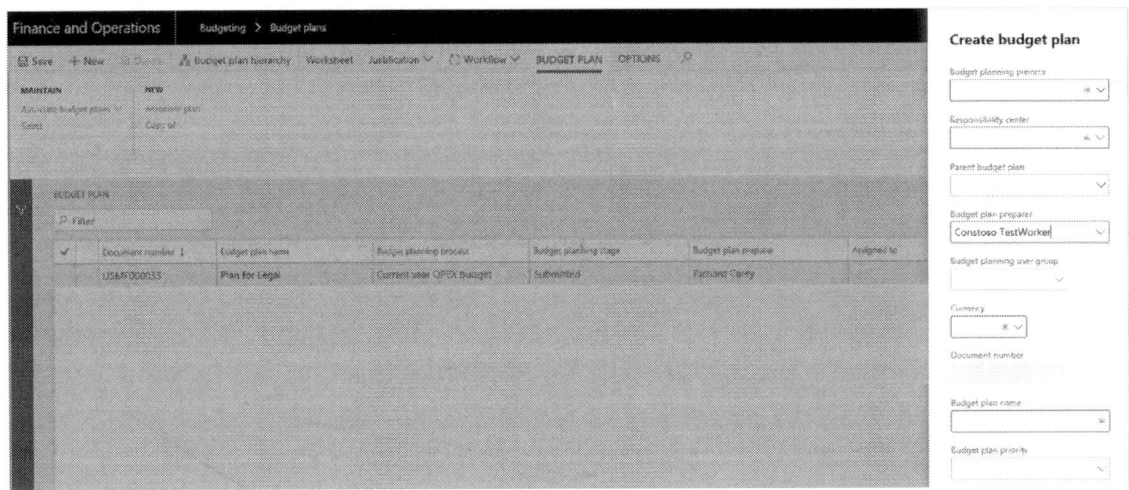

Create Budget Register Entries

1. From Budgeting open Budget register entries
    1. See MS docs 'Create budget register entries'
    2. Click new
    3. Apply register entries and add lines
        1. Note Open in excel option on action tab, for subsequent edits and updates
        2. Note budget model and code

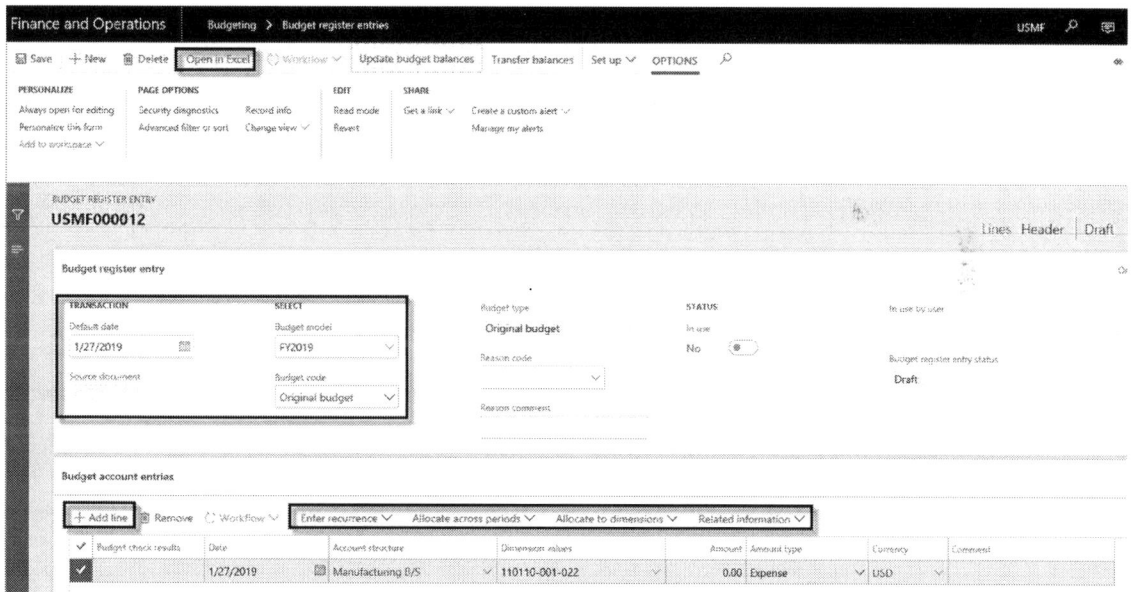

3. Register budget types can be defined using the Budget code form

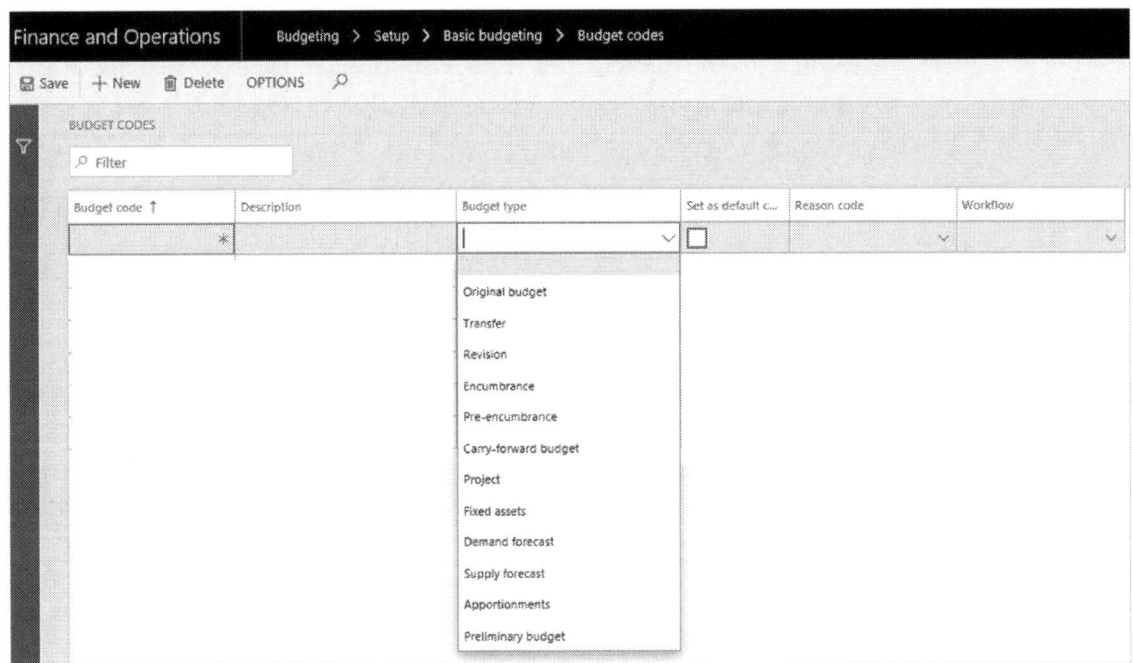

2. On the budget account entries fast tab add a line
   1. Note recurrence to set the same amount for each period
   2. Note allocation to allocate a % across periods

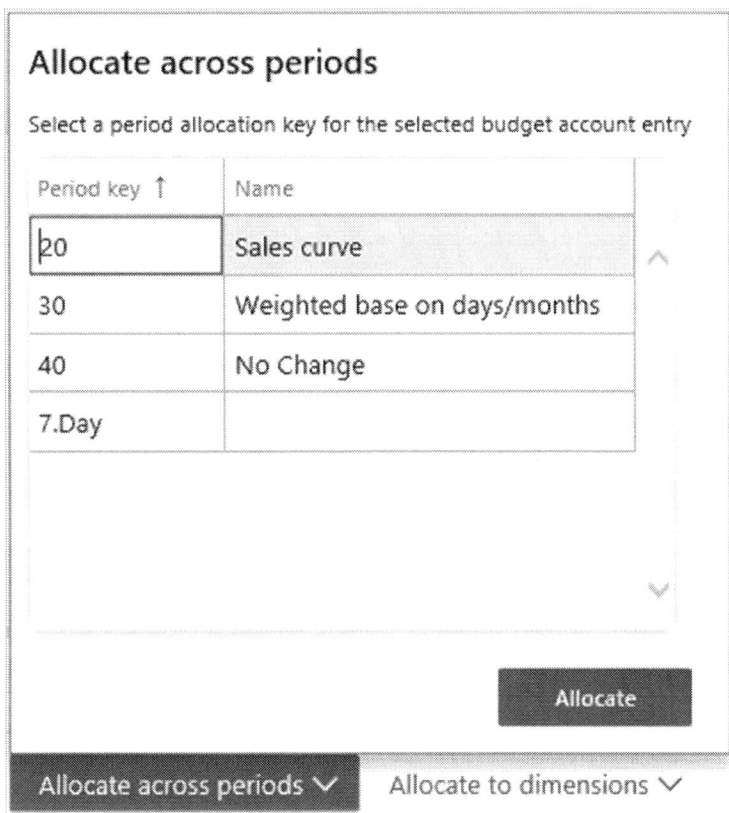

3. When done from the action tab click Update budget balances

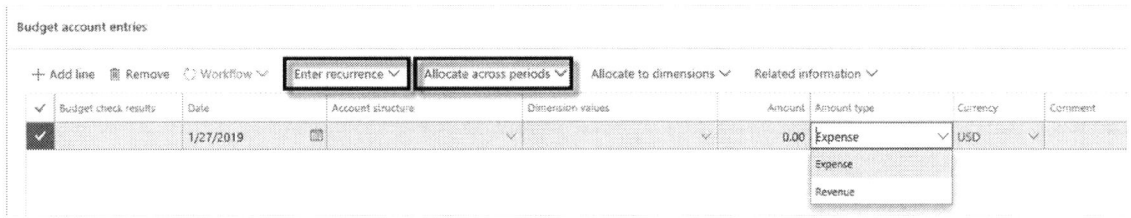

Commitment / Encumbrance Accounting

1. From <u>GL</u> open GL parameters
2. Commitment or encumbrance accounting manages the budget by setting aside budget funds.
3. Note MS Docs 'Encumber purchase orders' reference: When you create and confirm purchase orders with this process enabled, **a budget reservation is created to make sure that actual expenditures do not <u>exceed</u> the available budget**.
4. To enable encumbrance accounting
   1. Create an encumbrance account and posting definition
   2. Create an invoice posting definition
   3. Assign the encumbrance posting definition of the purchase order transaction posting type
   4. Assign the accounts payable posting invoice definition to the invoice transaction posting type
   5. Enable use of posting definitions and the encumbrance process in GL parameters

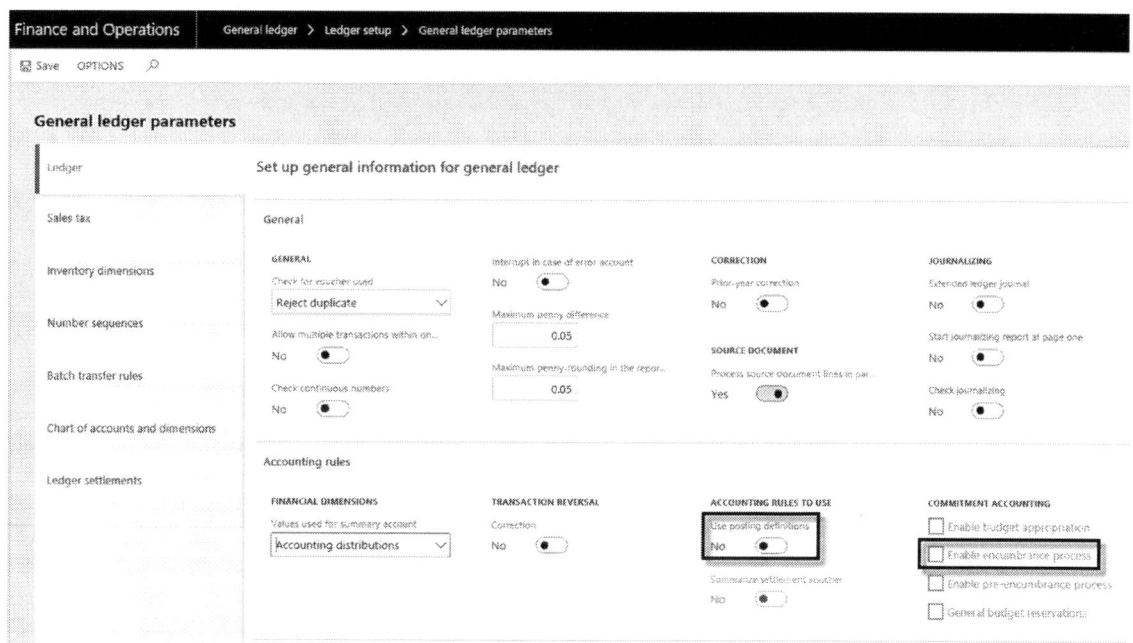

5. From <u>Budgeting</u> open Budget codes
6. Note the that encumbrance and pre-encumbrance definitions can be assigned via Budget codes

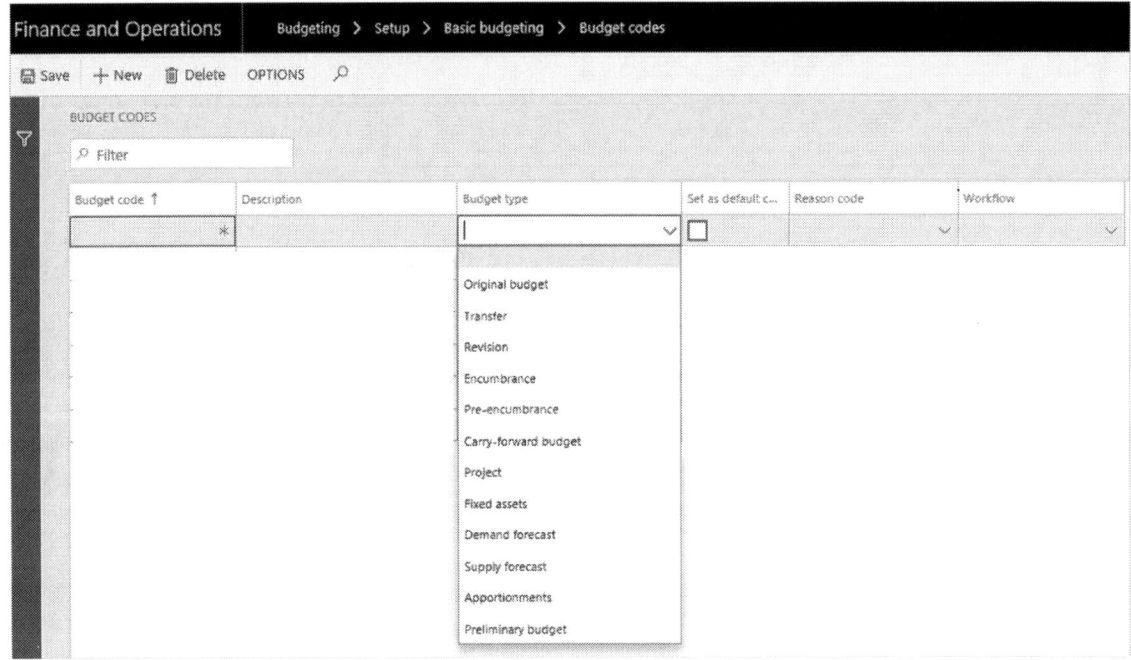

ACCOUNTS PAYABLE /

PROCUREMENT

Vendor Invoice Posting

1. From Accounts Payable, open the Invoice Register

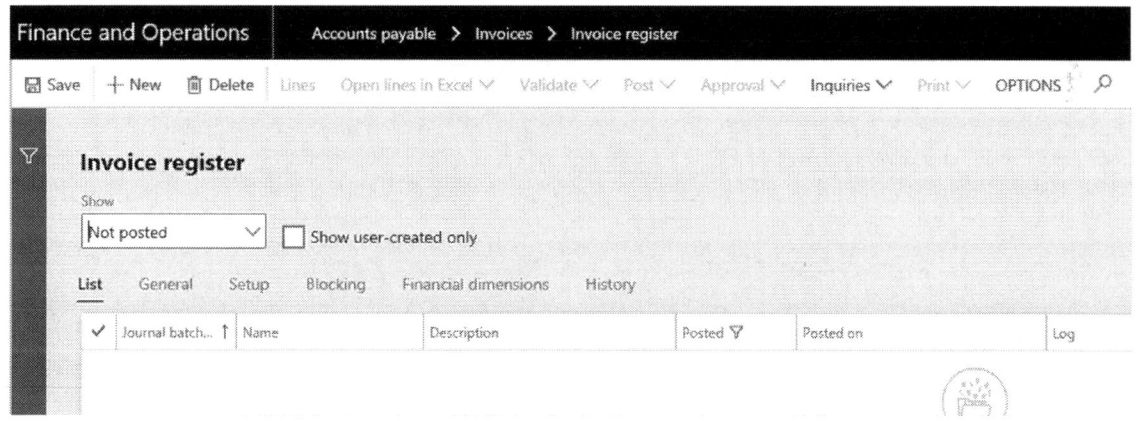

2. Click New and enter the journal line

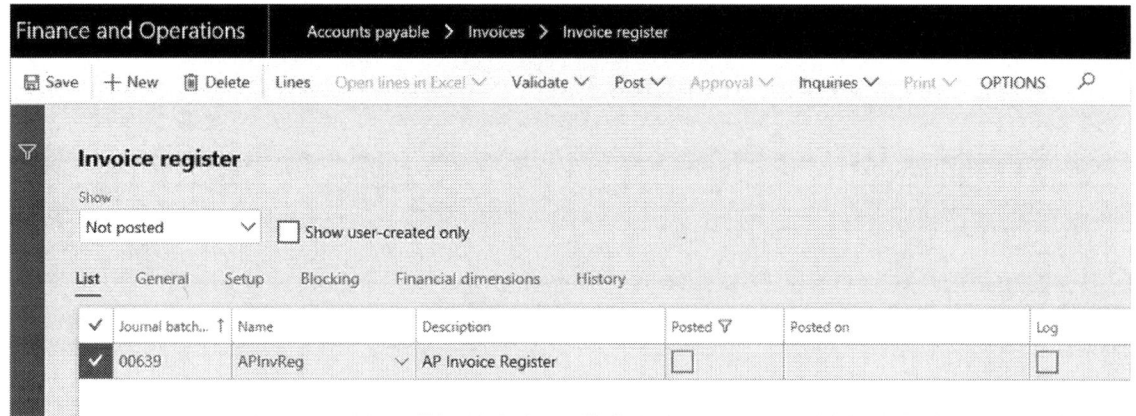

3. Click Lines and apply updates, including for the following entries
   1. Account
   2. Invoice
   3. Credit or Debit
   4. Approved by

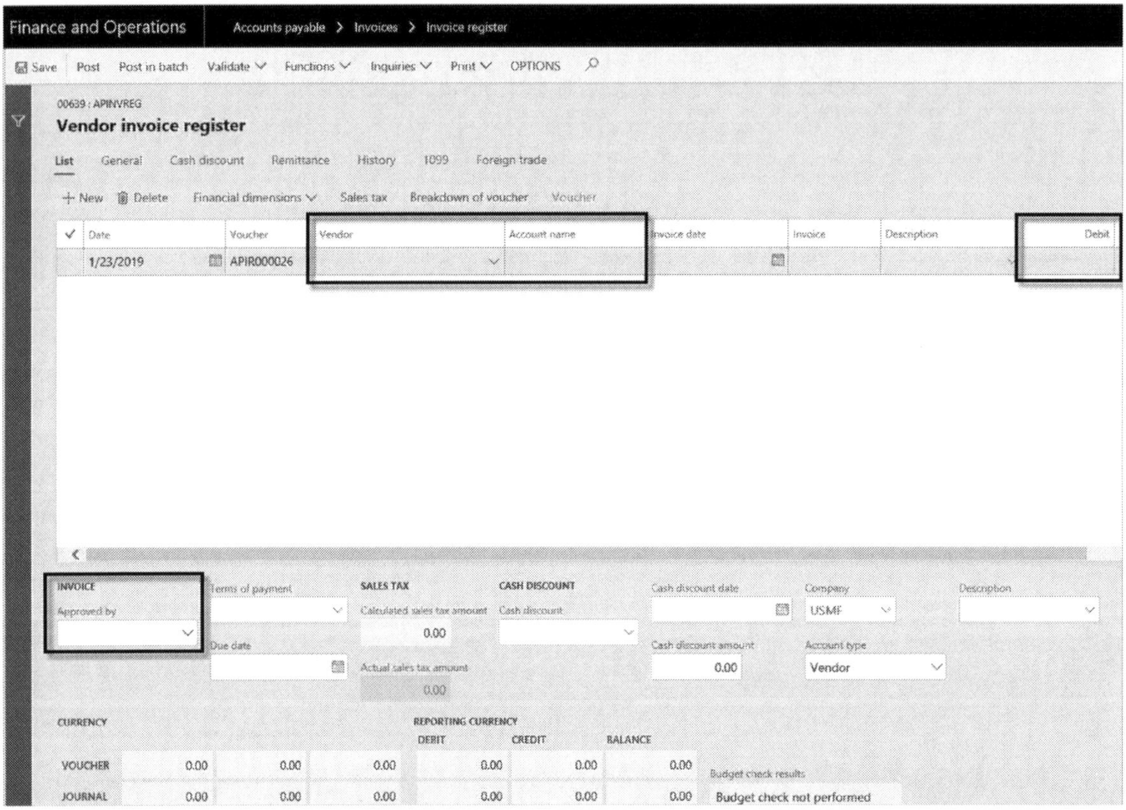

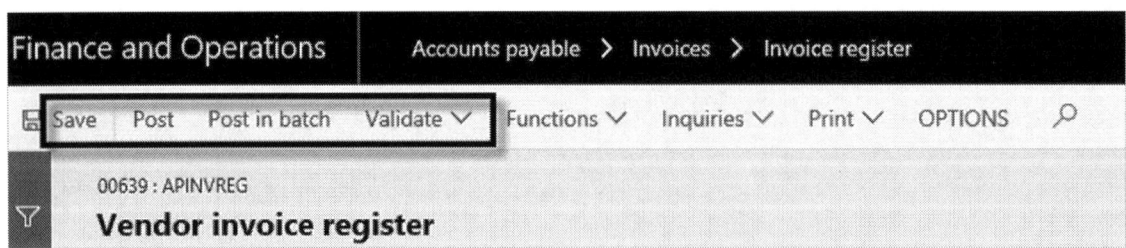

4. Save, Validate and Post

Matching

1. From Accounts Payable open Accounts Payable Parameters

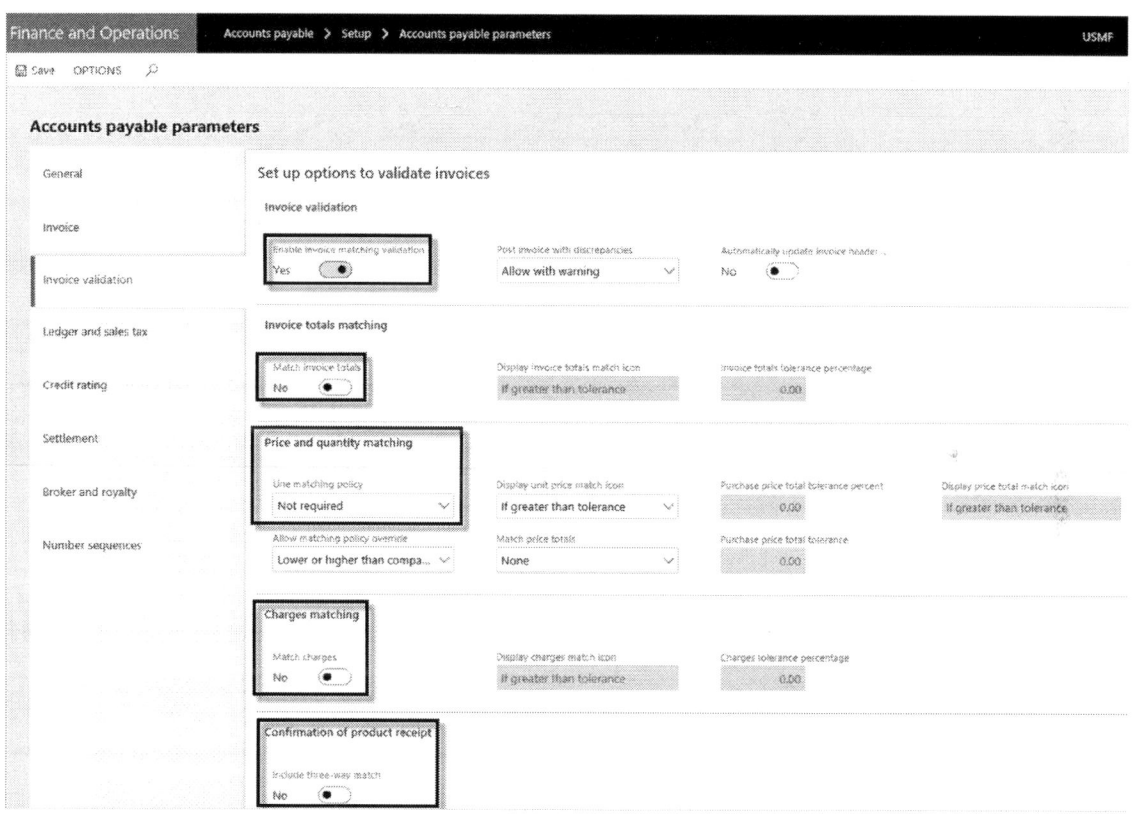

2.   Note matching options on the price and quantity fast tab

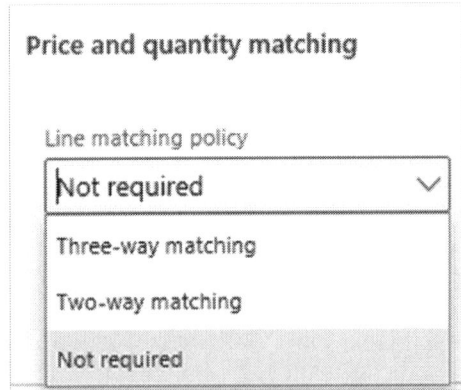

<u>Payment Schedules</u>

1.   From Accounts Payable open Payment Schedules

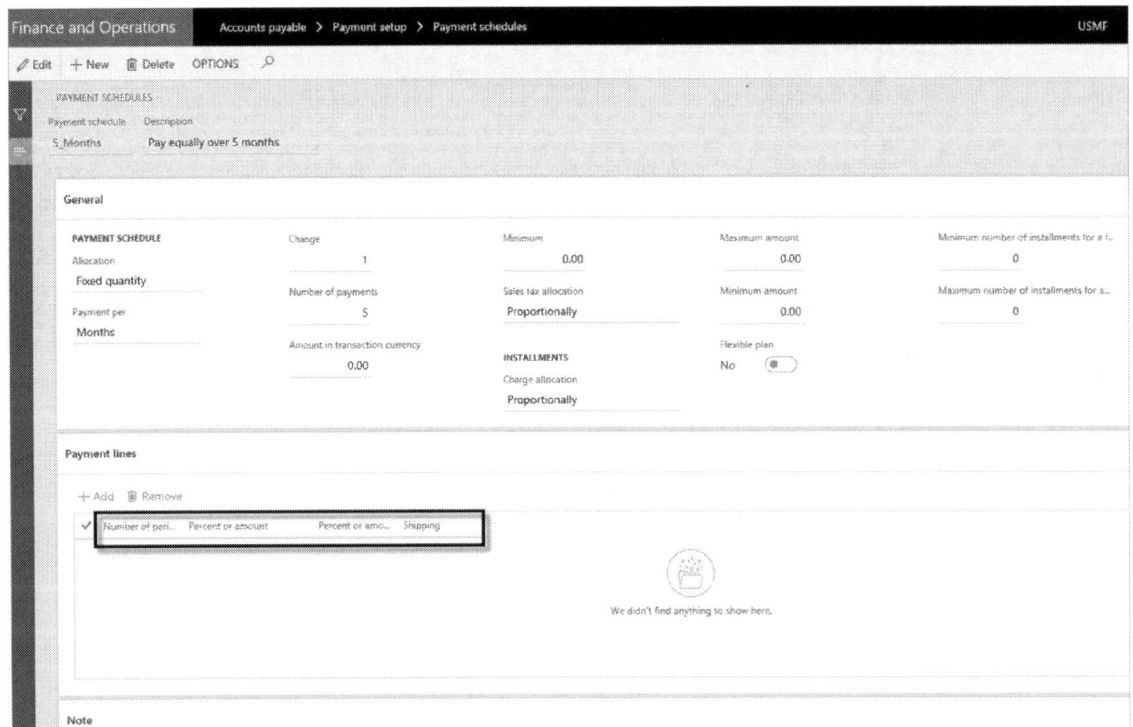

2. Schedules are used in conjunction with terms and days
   1. Setup terms from Accounts Payable, Terms of Payment
   2. Note that a payment schedule and/or day may be specified

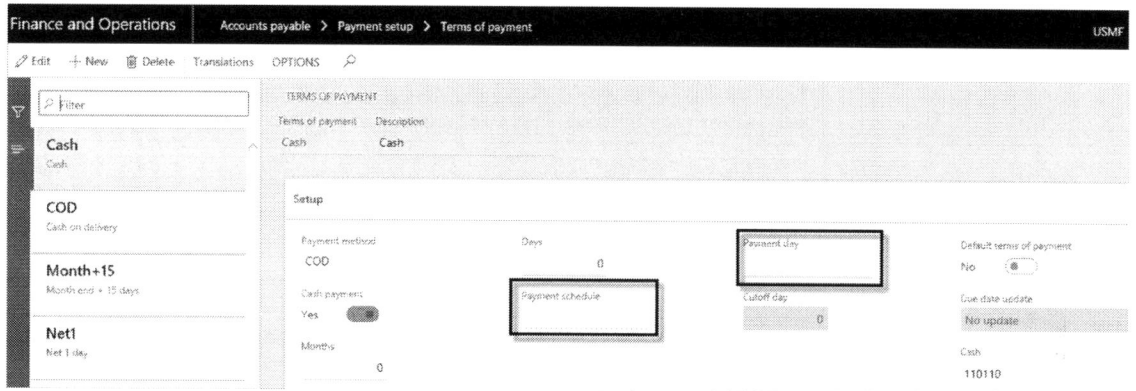

3. Setup days from Accounts Payable, Payment Days

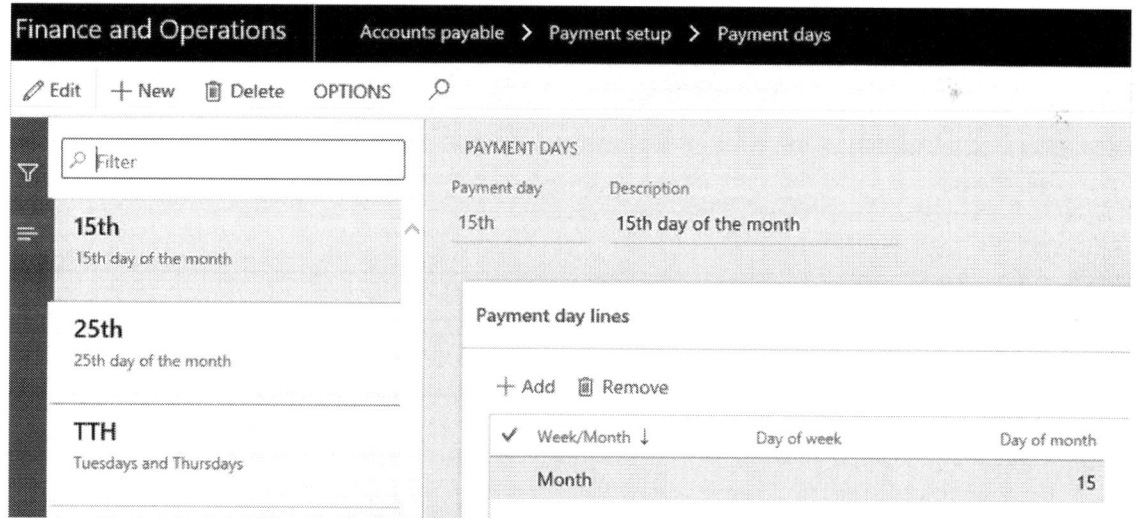

33

Payment Proposal

1. From Account Payable open Payment Journals
    1. See MS docs: 'Create vendor payments by using a payment proposal'
    2. Are used to quickly select vendor invoices for payment
    3. Click Lines

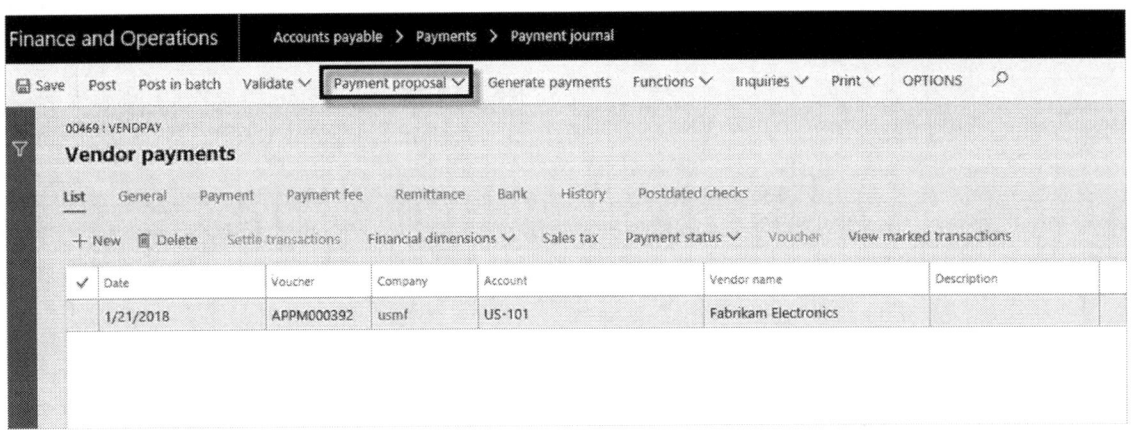

2. Select the Payment proposal drop down can click Create Payment Proposal
   1. Pop will provide filter and date criteria
   2. Click OK
   3. Remove payment/invoice lines if applicable
   4. Click Create payments at bottom of form
   5. System transfers proposal to journal

Vendor payment proposal

Invoices   Cash discount

🗑 Remove   Multiple change   Payment distribution   Balance control   Show payment overview

✓	Vendor name ↑	Invoice	Company accou...	Date to pay	Due date	Cash discount date	Cash discount a...	Amount to pay i...
	Acme Office Supplies	80193	usmf	2/9/2019	7/4/2017	6/14/2017	0.00	-4,589.10
	Acme Office Supplies	09310	usmf	2/9/2019	7/7/2017	6/17/2017	0.00	-782.09
	Acme Office Supplies		usmf	2/9/2019	6/12/2017		0.00	892.57
	Acme Office Supplies	309	usmf	2/9/2019	7/19/2017	7/4/2017	0.00	-309.03

3. Post

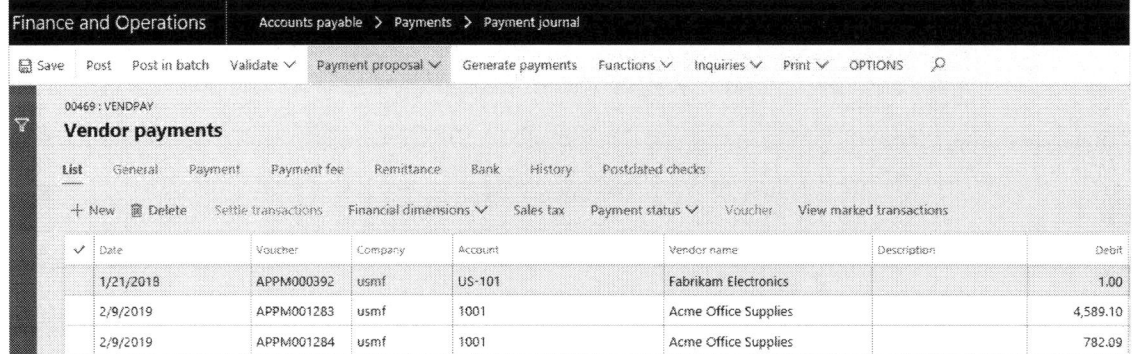

Finance and Operations   Accounts payable > Payments > Payment journal

🖫 Save   Post   Post in batch   Validate ∨   Payment proposal ∨   Generate payments   Functions ∨   Inquiries ∨   Print ∨   OPTIONS   🔍

00469 : VENDPAY
Vendor payments

List   General   Payment   Payment fee   Remittance   Bank   History   Postdated checks

+ New   🗑 Delete   Settle transactions   Financial dimensions ∨   Sales tax   Payment status ∨   Voucher   View marked transactions

✓	Date	Voucher	Company	Account	Vendor name	Description	Debit
	1/21/2018	APPM000392	usmf	US-101	Fabrikam Electronics		1.00
	2/9/2019	APPM001283	usmf	1001	Acme Office Supplies		4,589.10
	2/9/2019	APPM001284	usmf	1001	Acme Office Supplies		782.09

35

4. If payments are created manually, use the Settle transactions to select invoices for settlement (see MS docs: Settlement Overview)

 1. Note that while payment proposals are manually created, invoices are automatically marked for settlement when payments are created

 2. From Lines click Settle Transactions

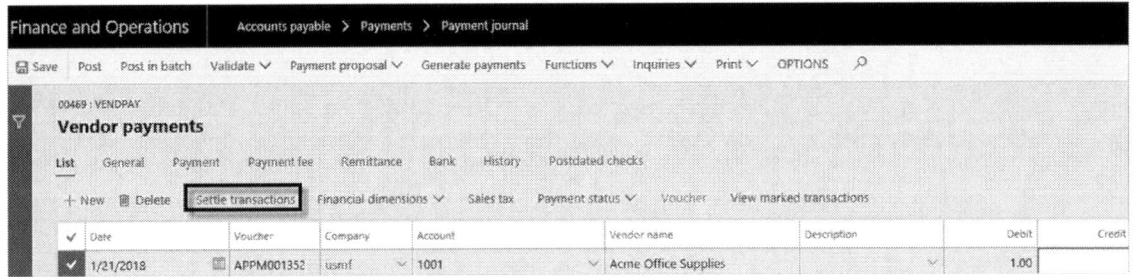

 3. Mark and click OK. Post.

Settle transactions for Acme Office Supplies

| Overview | General | Payment | Settlement | Remittance | Cash discount | Financial dimensions | Withholding tax |

Mark selected   Unmark all   Show marked ∨   Apply payment schedule

✓	Mark	Fully settle	Invoice	Due date	Cash discount date	Amount	Currency	Amount to settle	Amount to settl...
	☐	☐	10017	7/30/2017	7/30/2017	378.09	USD	-378.09	-378.09
	☐	☐	10012	7/28/2017	7/28/2017	23,109.90	USD	-23,109.90	-23,109.90
	☐	☐	100189	7/23/2017	7/23/2017	7,209.98	USD	-7,209.98	-7,209.98

Create Vendor Invoice

1. From Accounts Payable open Payment register
2. If an invoice is not connected to a PO, invoices can be entered via the following:
    1. Vendor invoice register
        1. Invoice pools are often used with invoice registers (see MS docs 'Key invoice data into the AP system using invoice pool')
        2. Note approved by field

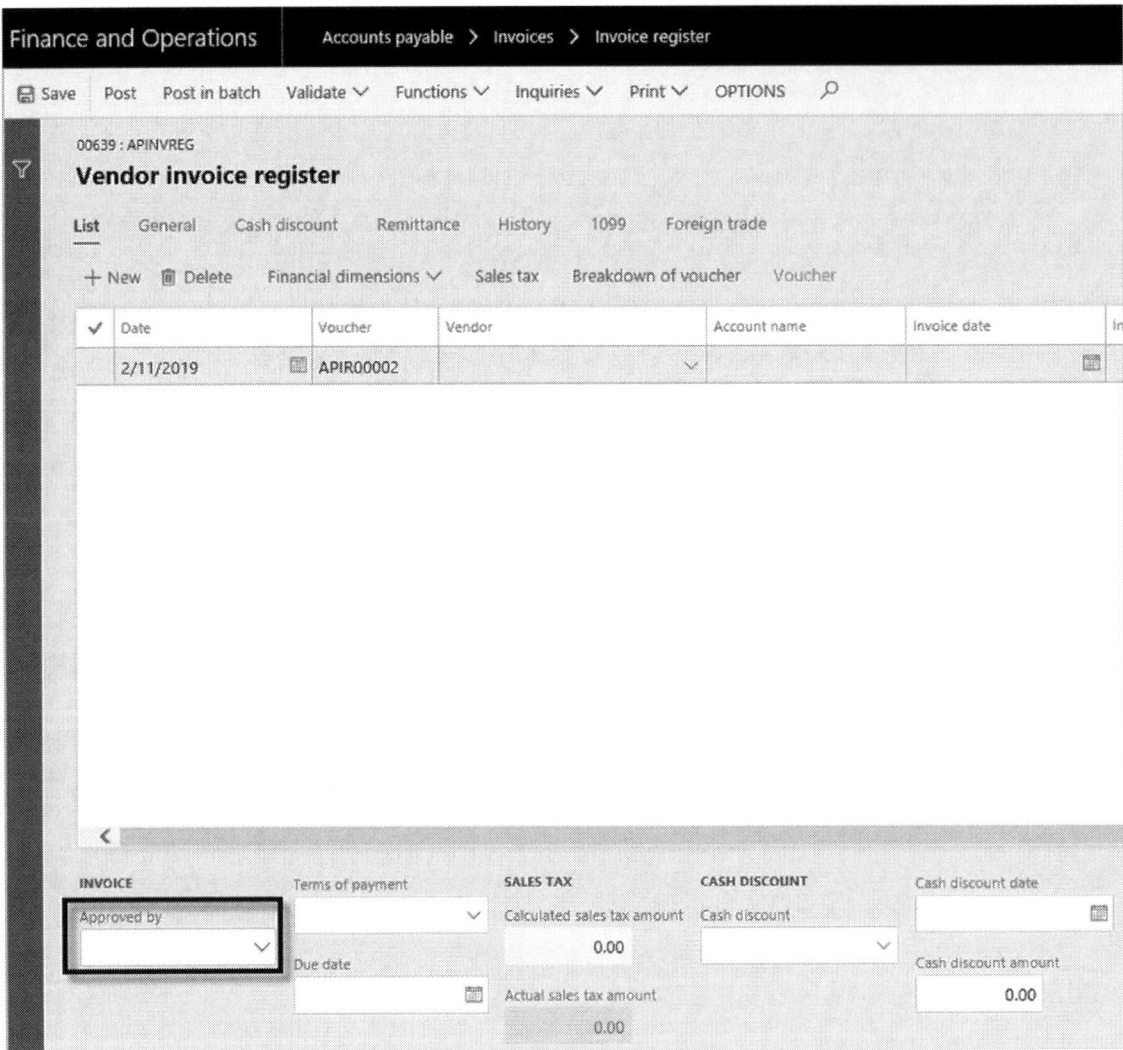

2.   From AP open Vendor invoice Journal

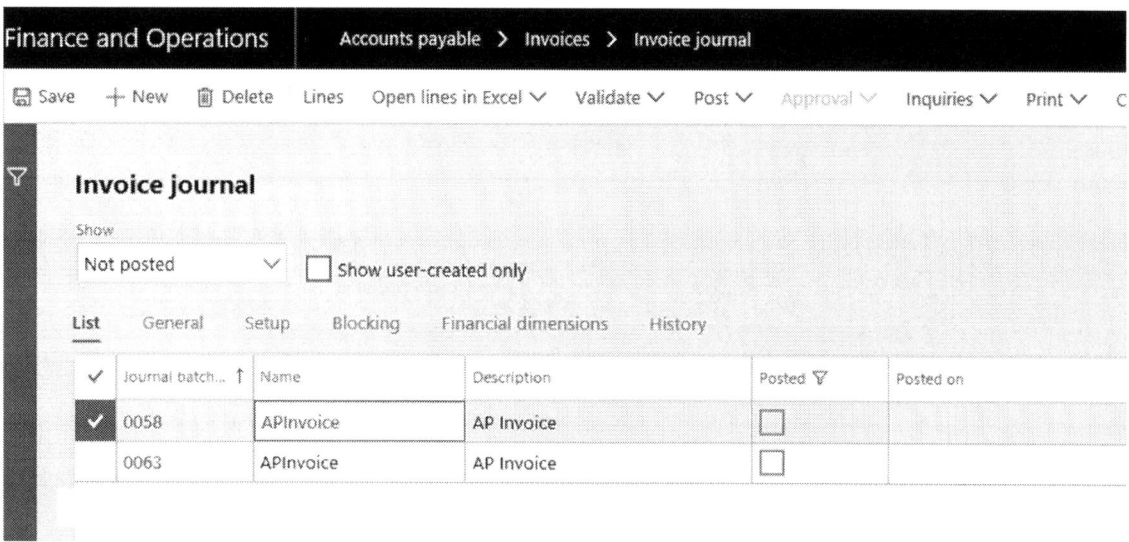

3.   From AP open Vendor invoice approval journal
   1.   For subsequent approval of a register or invoice journal
          entry

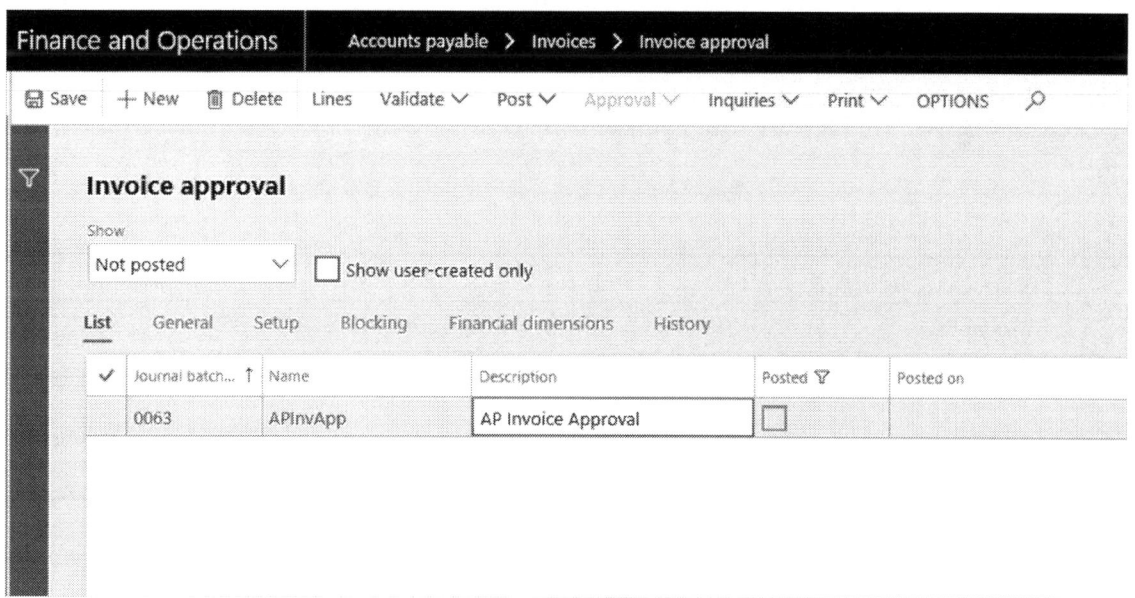

Vendor Groups

1. From Procurement and Sourcing open Vendor Groups
    1. Note group parameters
        1. Terms
        2. Time between
        3. Default tax

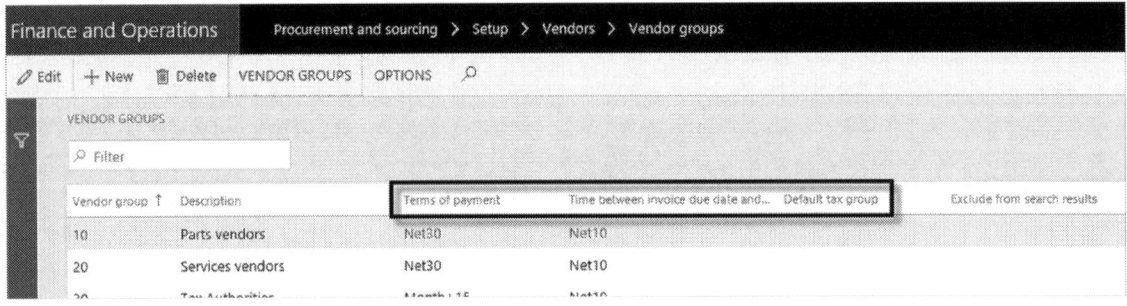

ACCOUNTS RECEIVABLE / SALES

and MARKETING

Customer Invoices

1. From Accounts Receivable open All Sales Orders

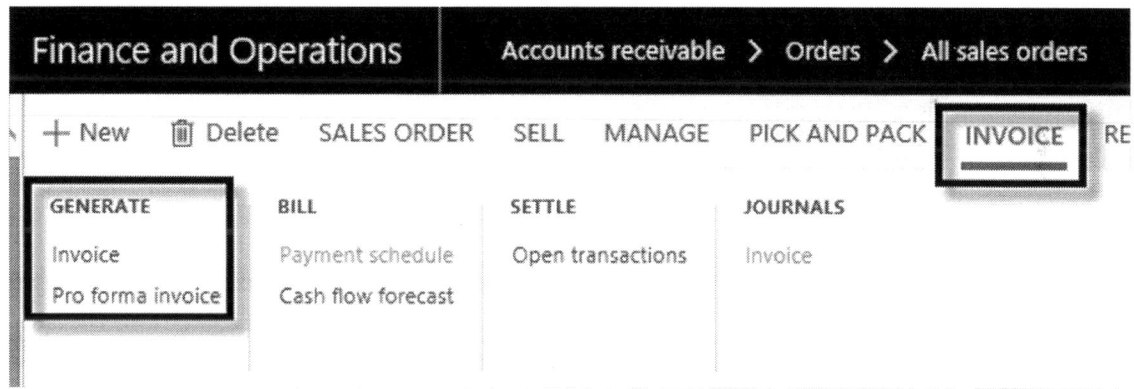

1.   Invoice

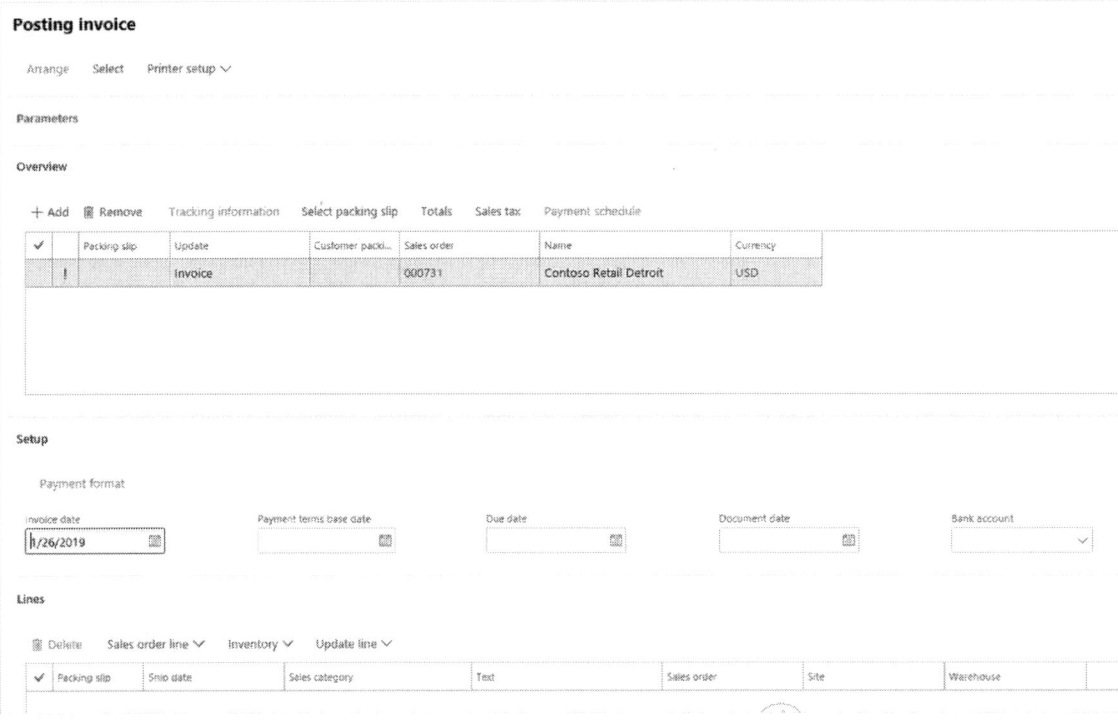

2.   SO Pro Forma (used for estimations)

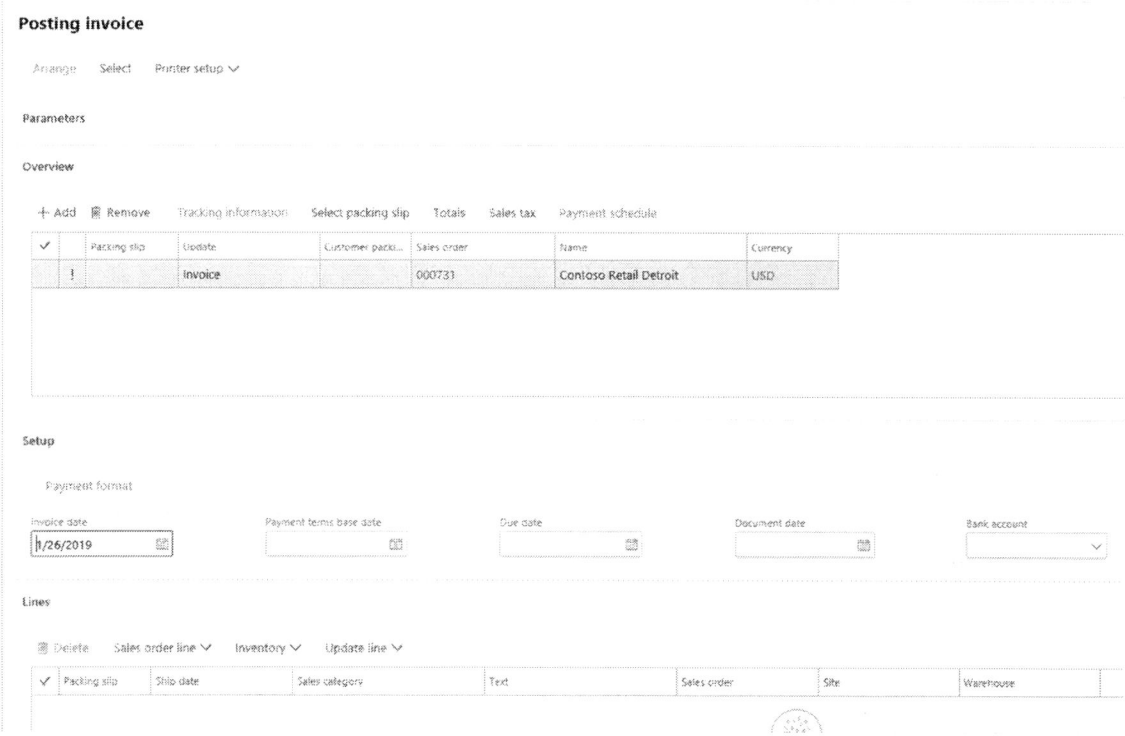

Posting invoice

Arrange   Select   Printer setup ∨

Parameters

Overview

+ Add   Remove   Tracking information   Select packing slip   Totals   Sales tax   Payment schedule

✓	Packing slip	Update	Customer packi...	Sales order	Name	Currency
!		Invoice		000731	Contoso Retail Detroit	USD

Setup

Payment format

Invoice date	Payment terms base date	Due date	Document date	Bank account
1/26/2019				

Lines

Delete   Sales order line ∨   Inventory ∨   Update line ∨

✓	Packing slip	Ship date	Sales category	Text	Sales order	Site	Warehouse

43

2. Free Text Invoice
    1. Open All free text invoices
    2. For invoices <u>not</u> related to a sales order

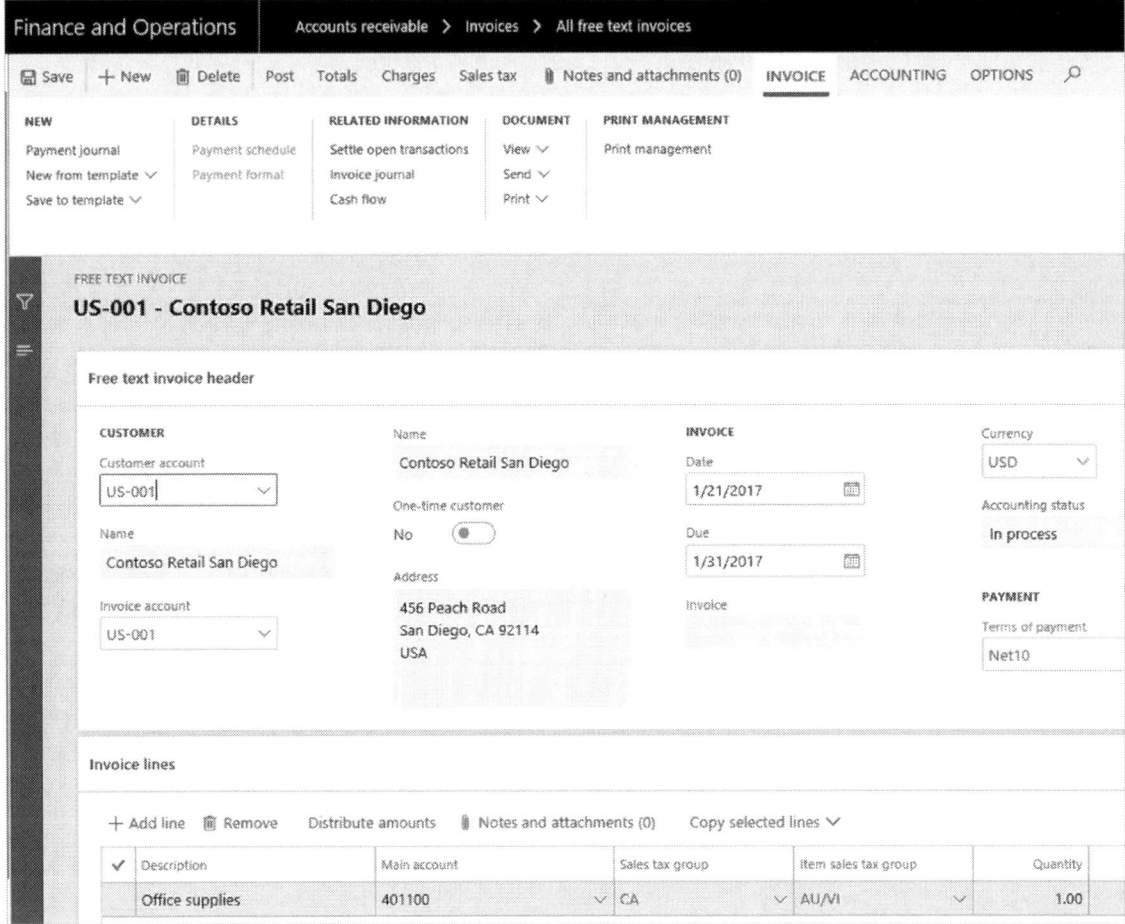

3.   Free Text Pro-forma (used for estimations)
    1.   Click Post

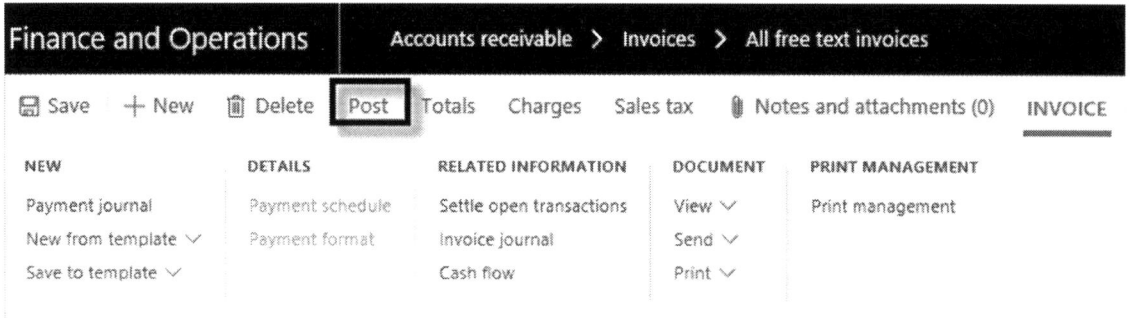

2.   Clear posting check box and click Print

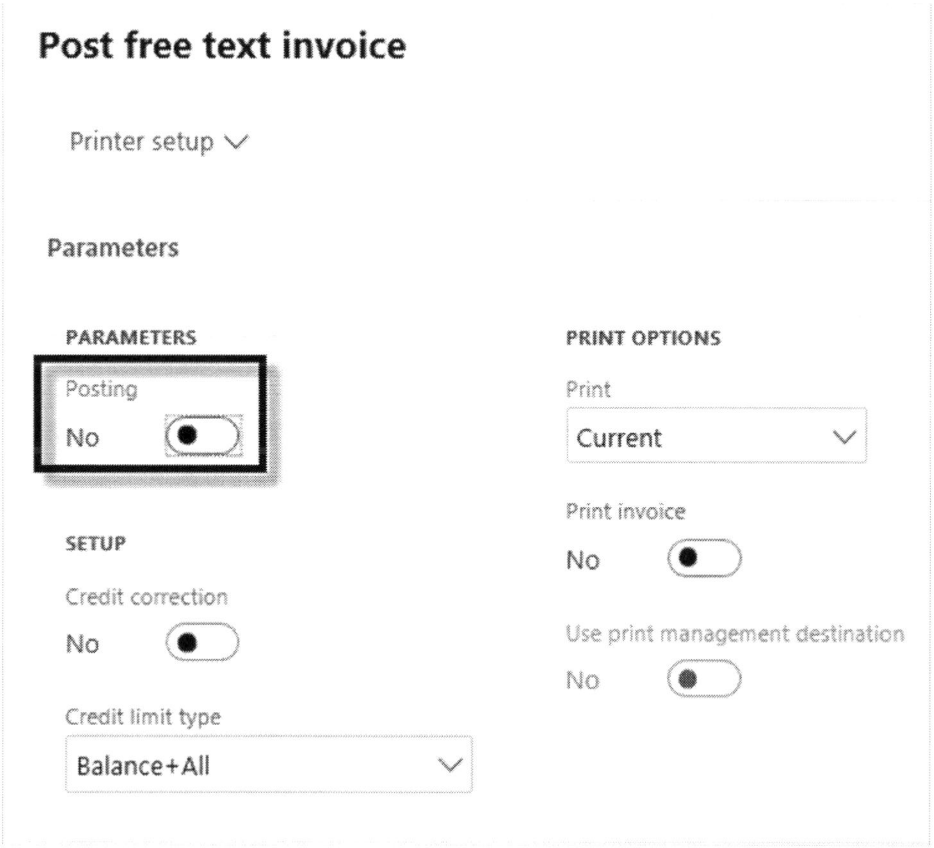

Post free text invoice

Printer setup ∨

Parameters

PARAMETERS

Posting

No ●⬤

SETUP

Credit correction

No ⬤●

Credit limit type

Balance+All ∨

PRINT OPTIONS

Print

Current ∨

Print invoice

No ⬤●

Use print management destination

No ●⬤

45

Create Deposit Slips

1.   From Accounts Receivable open Payment Journal
      1.   Click New

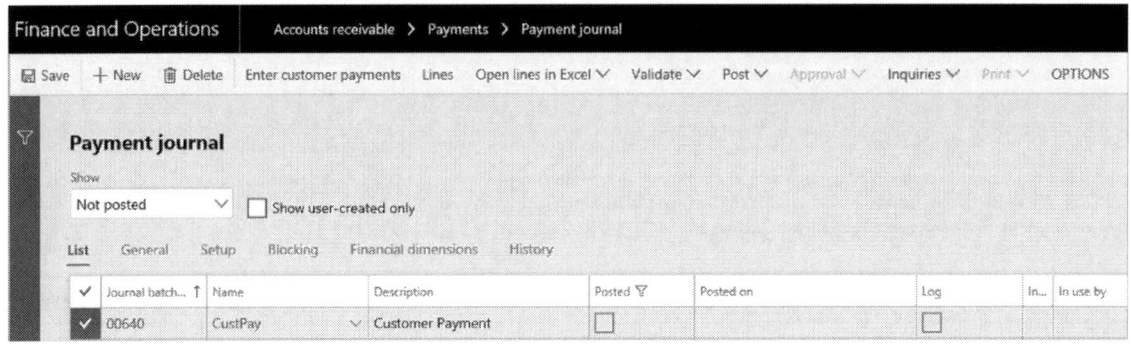

2.   Click Lines
      1.   Click Use Deposit Slip
      2.   Enter method of payment for the bank account
            1.   Note Payments tab
      3.   Repeat if required

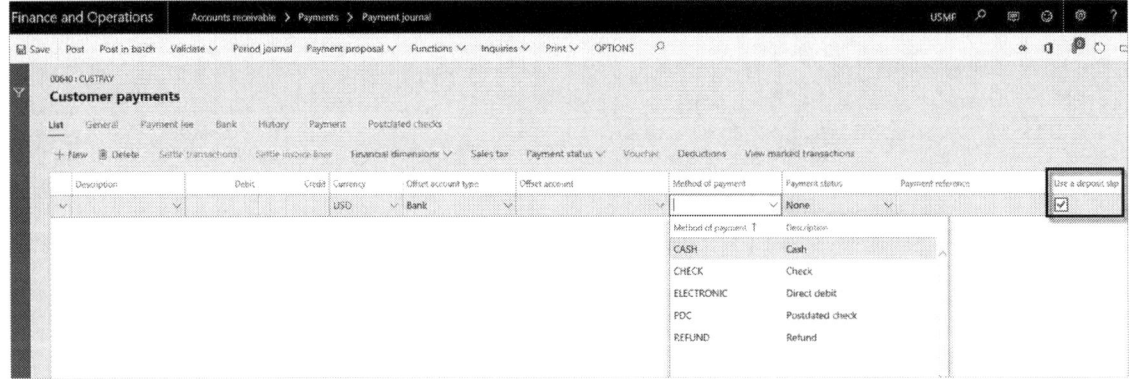

Payment Journal Bridging Account

1.   From Accounts Receivable open Methods of Payment
     1.   GL example. AP and AR methods also exist.
     2.   Note bridging posting is enabled, and account populated
     3.   Invoice update is typically set to automatic. This clears the invoice as paid as soon as an invoice is issued.

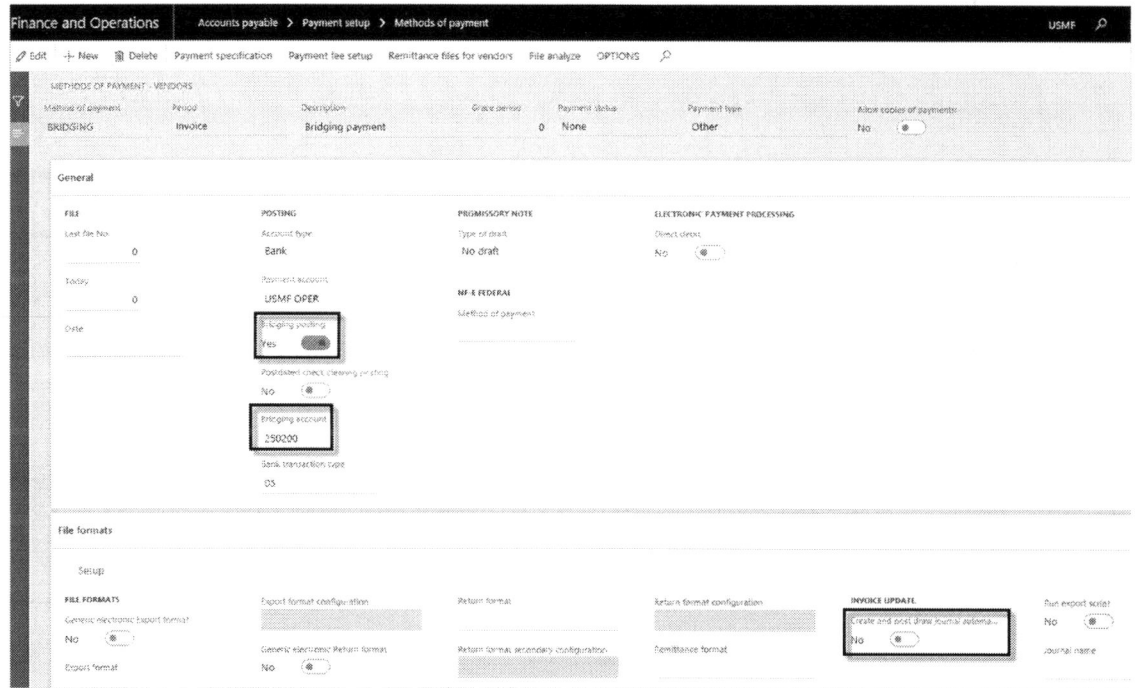

2.   From GL open General Journals and click Lines
1.   Click Select bridged transactions

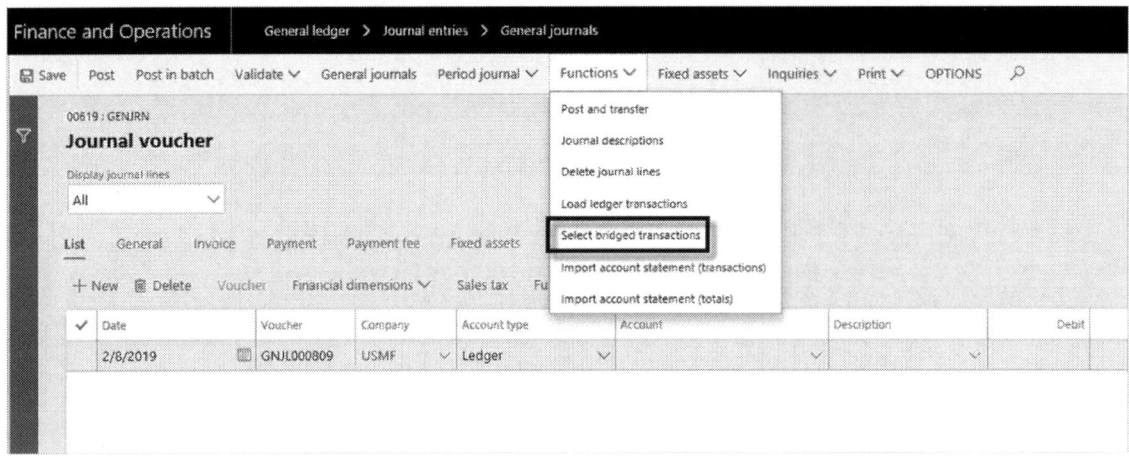

3.   Select relevant transactions and click Accept and post

4.   Post

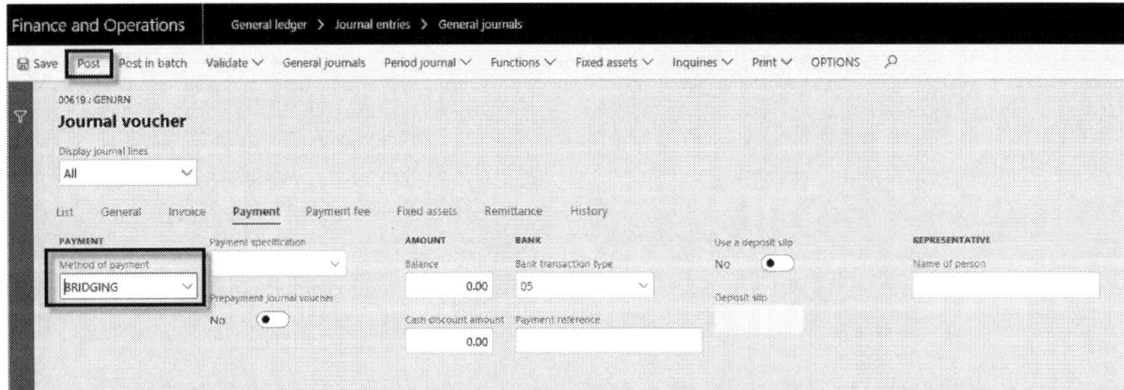

Customer Check Payments

1.   From Accounts Receivable open Payment Journals
   1.   Click new

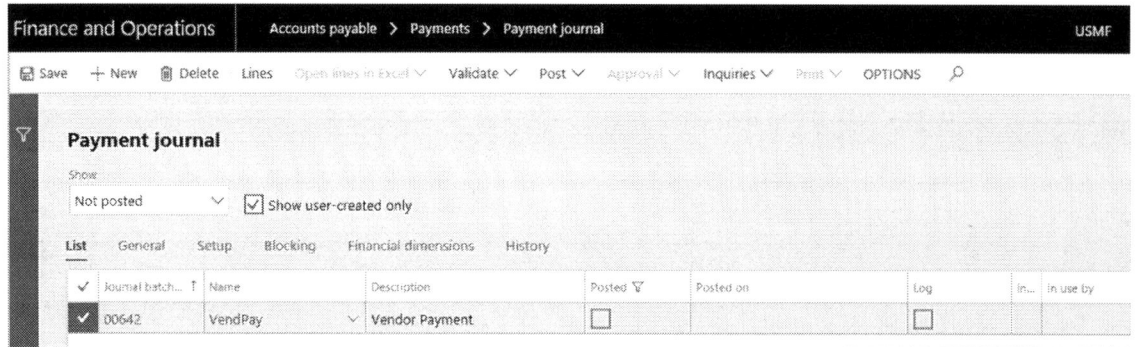

2.   Click Lines
   1.   Note Method of Payment

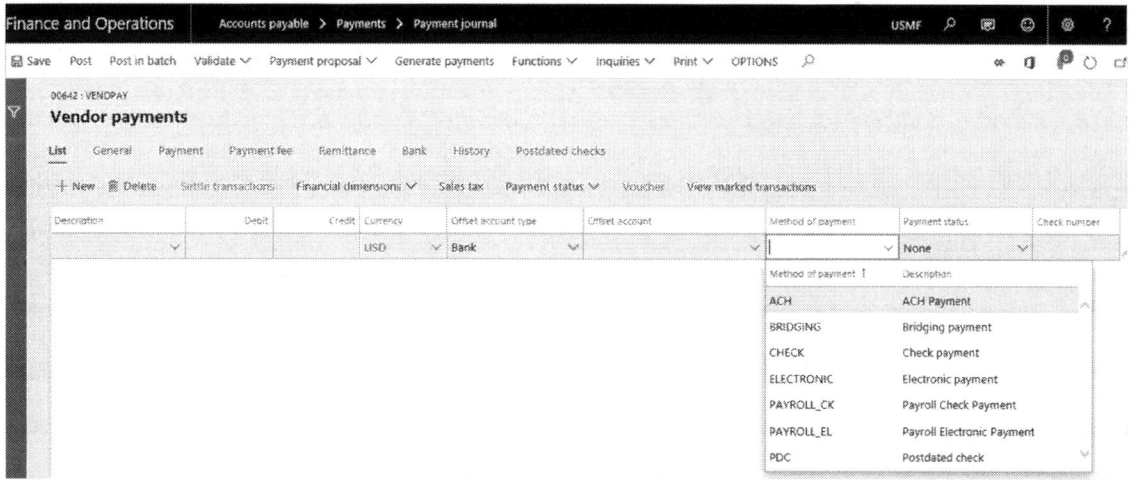

49

3. Note Payment Status, including Rejected to **void** an <u>unposted</u> check

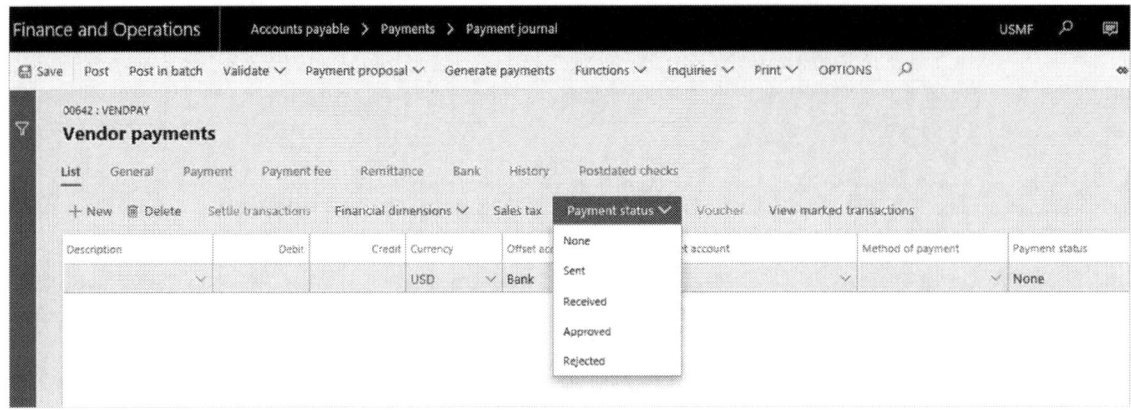

4. To **REUSE** the number of an unposted check
   1. Note Cash and bank management parameters needs the allow check reuse button set to Yes
      1. Note setting is available only to US and CAN entities

   2. From the Payment Journal on a check payment at status = Sent
      1. Click Payment Status drop down and click Reuse
      2. Payment status will be set back to None and check number field will be cleared
      3. Payment is ready to be regenerated

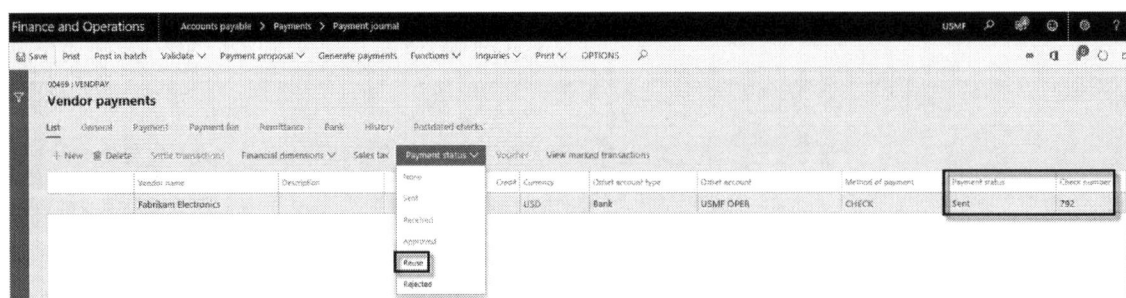

5.   To **REVERSE** a check
     1.   Note Cash and Bank Management parameters, Use review process for payments reversals is set to no

     1.   If set to yes use the Check Reversals under Payment reversal approvals

     2.   Click payment reversal

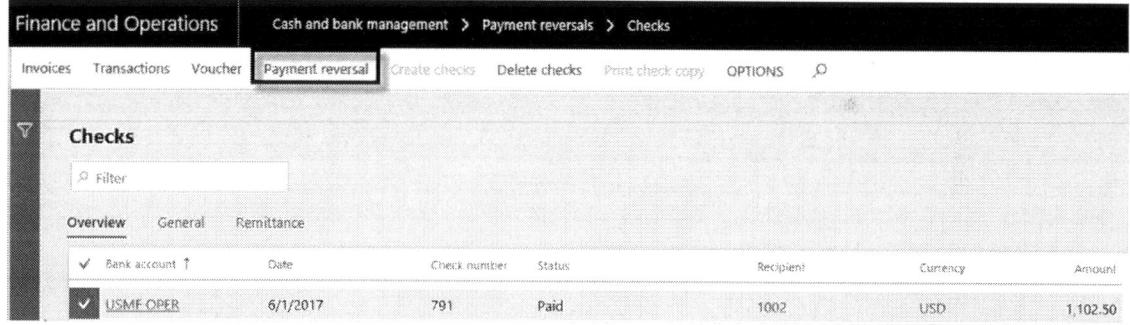

6.   The general rule of thumb is:
     1.   Reverse if posted
     2.   Delete if status is at 'created'
     3.   Void if unposted
     4.   Reject to change payment status (for void or rejected)

Customer Groups

1. From Sales and Marketing open Customer Groups
    1. Note input settings

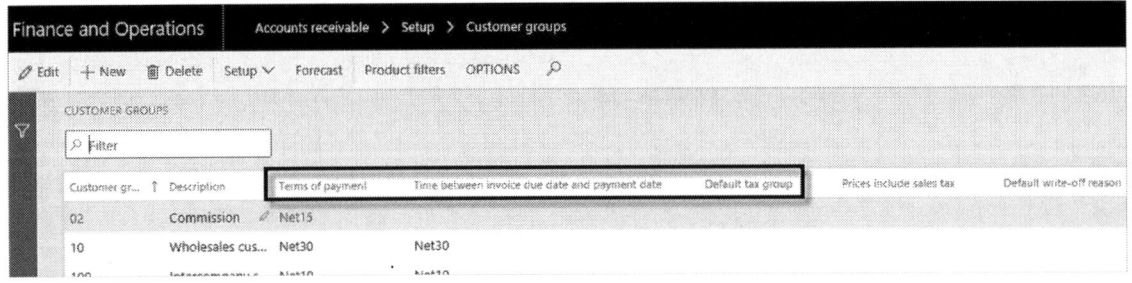

GENERAL LEDGER

Consolidation Overview

1. From MS docs 'Consolidation and elimination overview':
   1. When consolidating data, the financial results for multiple subsidiary companies are combined into results for a single, consolidated company. Subsidiaries might use different currencies.
   2. There are multiple options for consolidating data:
      1. From Consolidations open Consolidate online – This option consolidates daily balances by the selected accounts and dimensions, and stores them in a consolidation company.
      2. Financial reporting – This option enables consolidation of transactions and balances. Multiple levels of hierarchies can be created.
         1. Organization hierarchies that have legal entities or financial dimensions in them can be reviewed in financial reporting. Multilevel hierarchies can also be created by using a reporting tree definition that has a combination of legal entities and dimension values.
      3. Consolidate with import – This option imports balances into a consolidation company.
      4. Export company balances – Is used to provide an export file of company balances. The file can then be imported into other systems.

2.	From General Ledger open Financial dimensions
	1.	Note Dimension values (and Group dimension)
	2.	Note Hierarchy set up

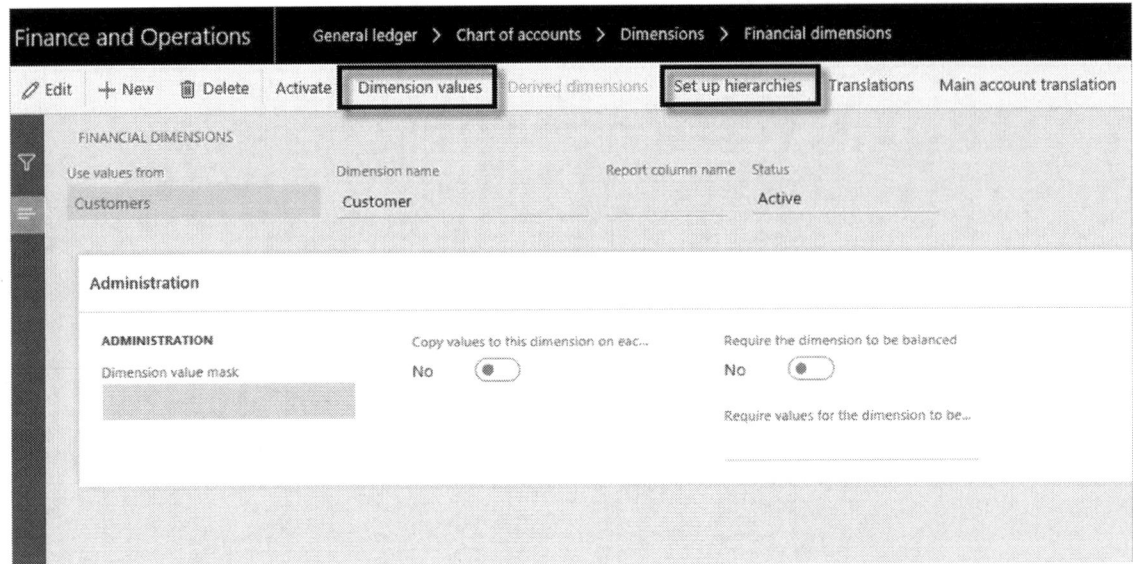

3.	Dimension values

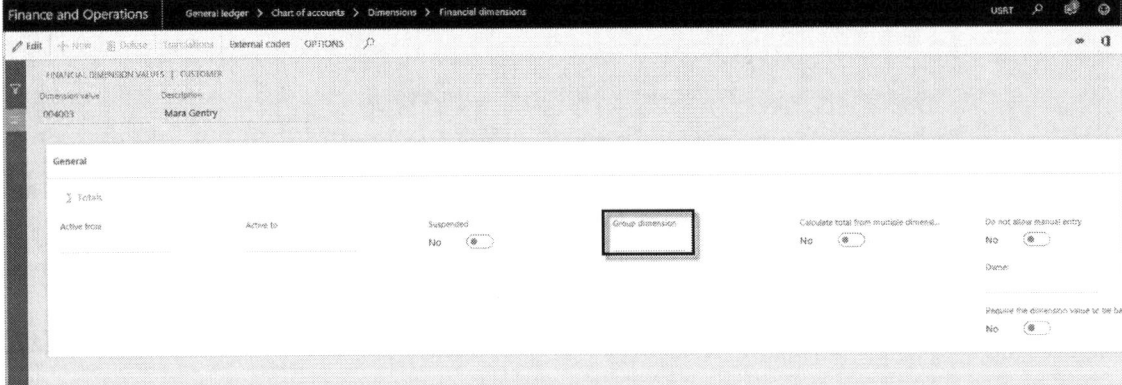

1. Group dimension

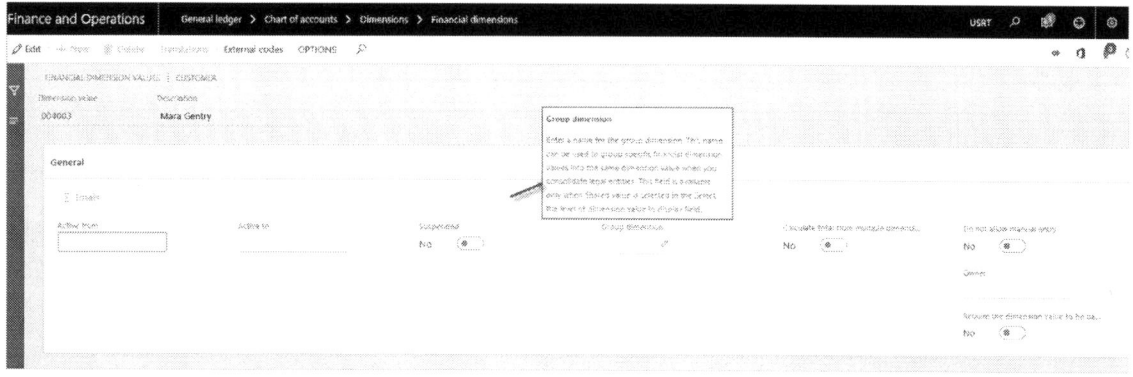

2. Hierarchy set up
   1. Note, association must be made for a derived financial hierarchy

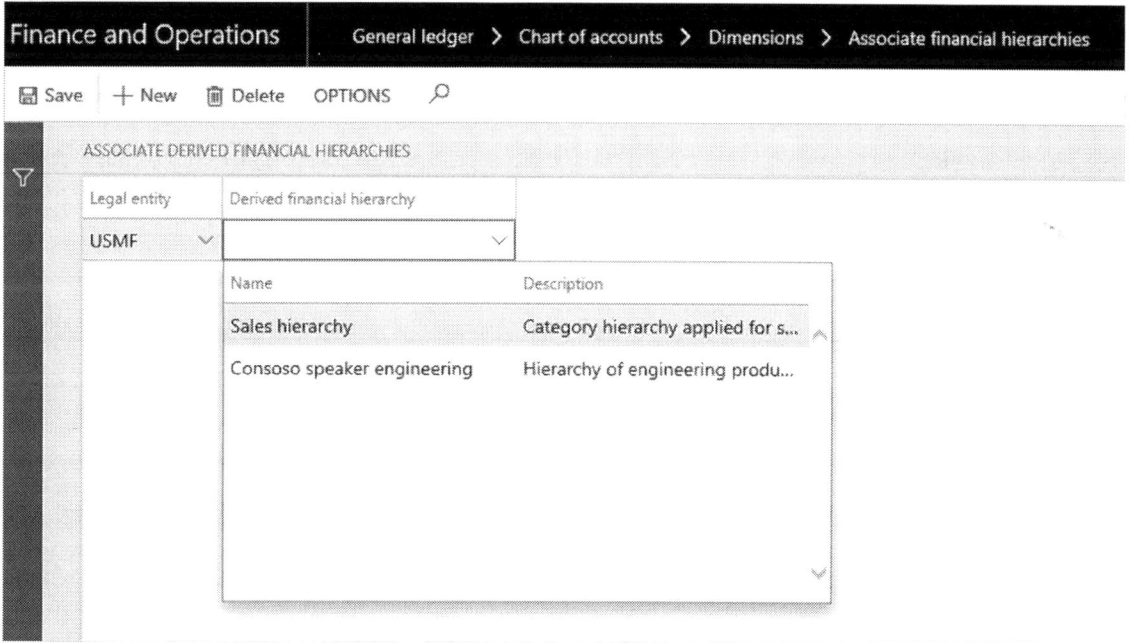

2.   With the association, derived can be selected

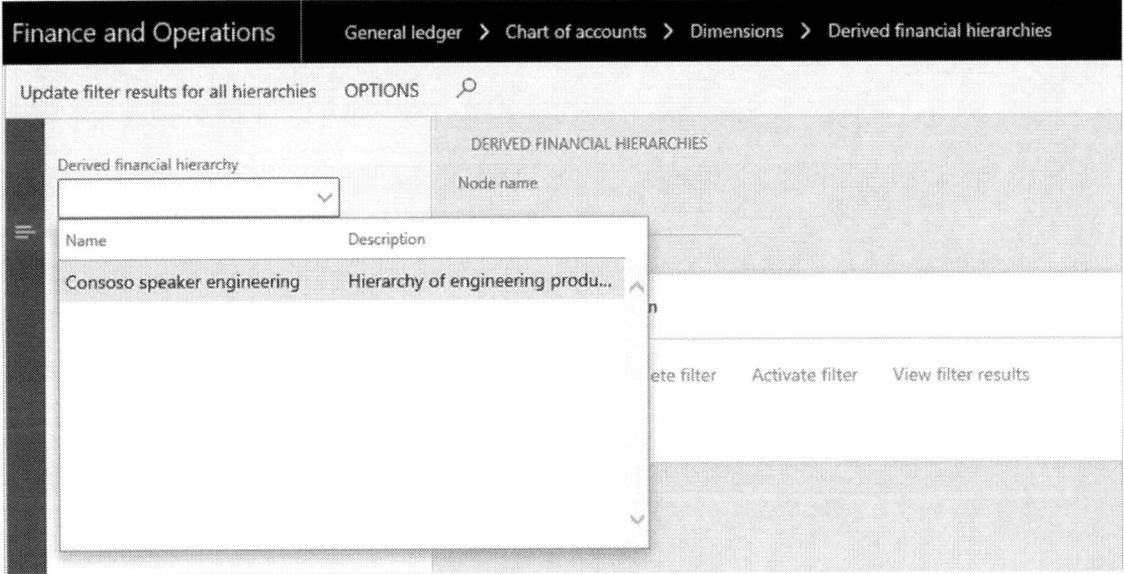

Consolidation Account Groups and Additional Consolidation Accounts

1.   Menu: General Ledger Chart of Accounts > Accounts

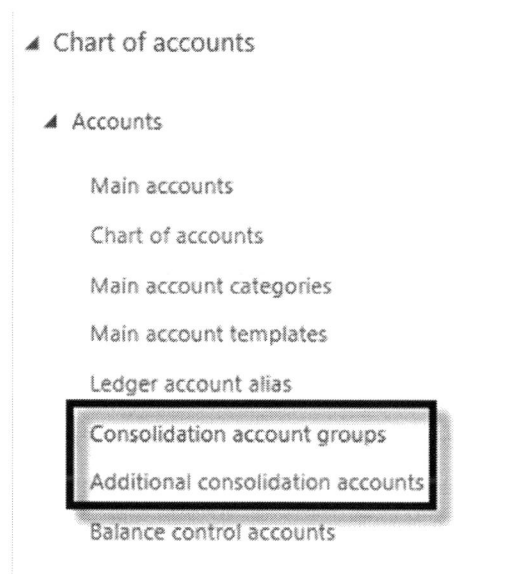

2.   From GL open Consolidation account groups
       1.   Consolidation accounts are typically used to consolidate data, often for a government mandated chart of accounts, or a headquarter consolidation.
       2.   Input value

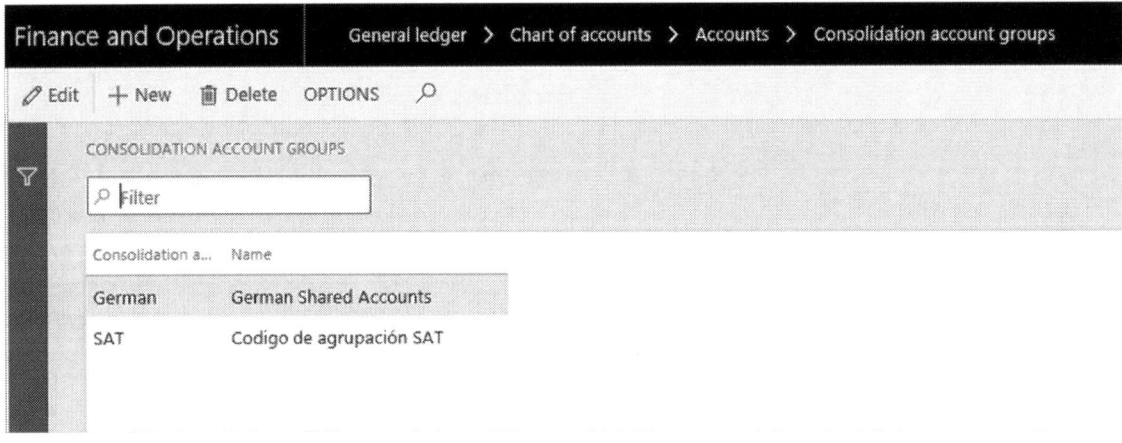

3.   Open Additional consolidation accounts
      1.   Click new and input
          1.   Main account (hyperlinked)
              1.   Note currency, which is set on the main account, and the use of which is also impacted by the consolidation account group setting
          2.   Consolidation account group
          3.   Consolidation account
          4.   Consolidation account name
          5.   SAT level (MX tax)

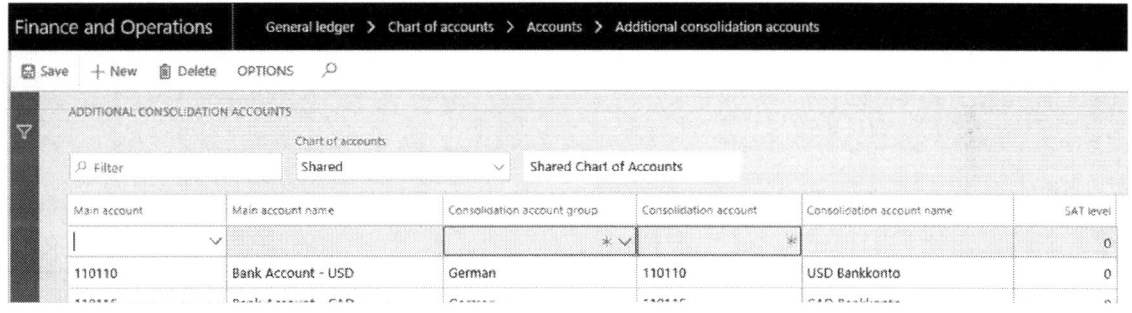

Consolidations and Legal Entities

1.   From <u>Organization Administration</u> open Legal Entities
    1.   Enable Use for financial consolidation process
        1.   If set to Yes, some or all applicable balances are moved to the consolidation account
    2.   Elimination process is also relevant but is not covered in this section
    3.   If the entity is new, related number sequences will also need to be generated.

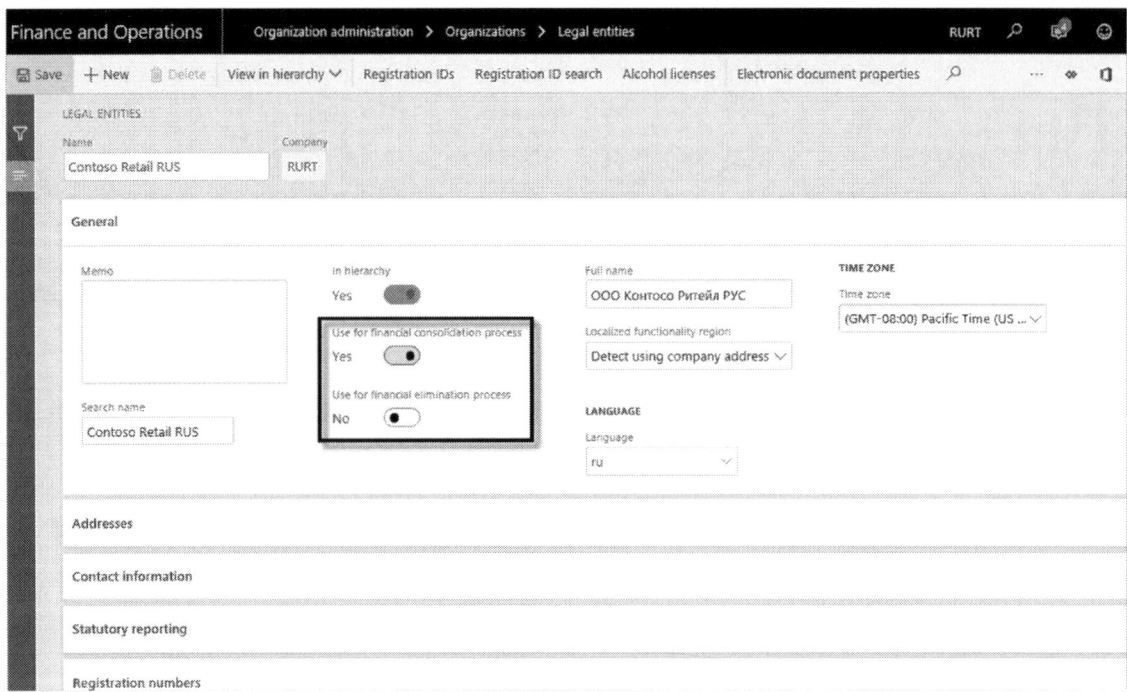

2. From General Ledger open Ledger
    1. At a minimum apply
        1. Chart of accounts
        2. Fiscal calendar
        3. Accounting currency
        4. Default exchange rate type

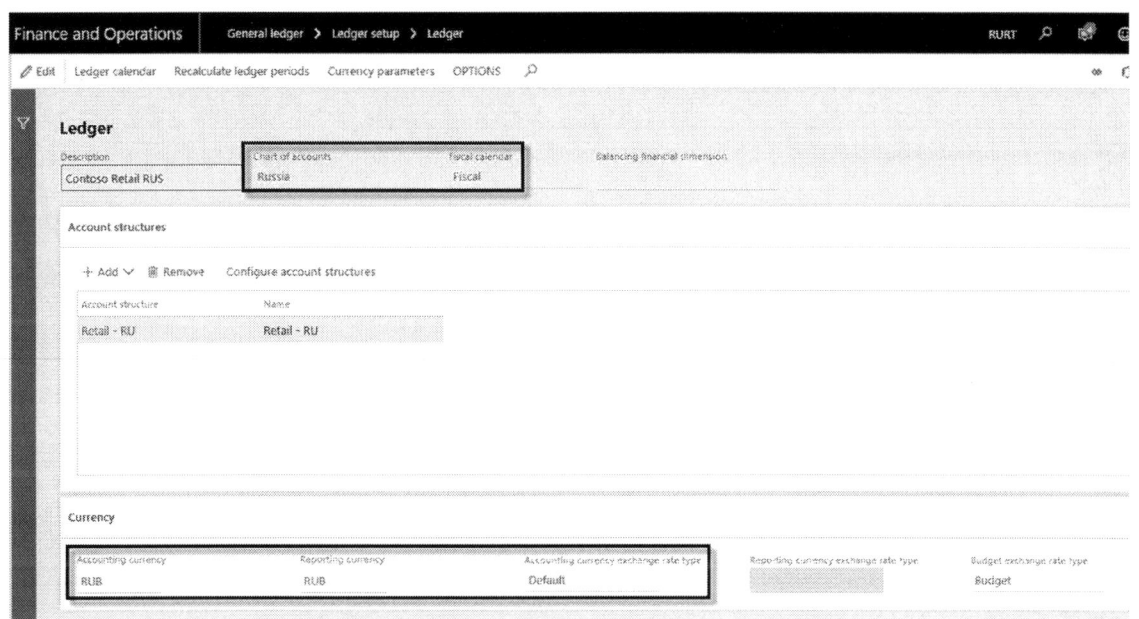

3.   From General Ledger open Currency exchange rates

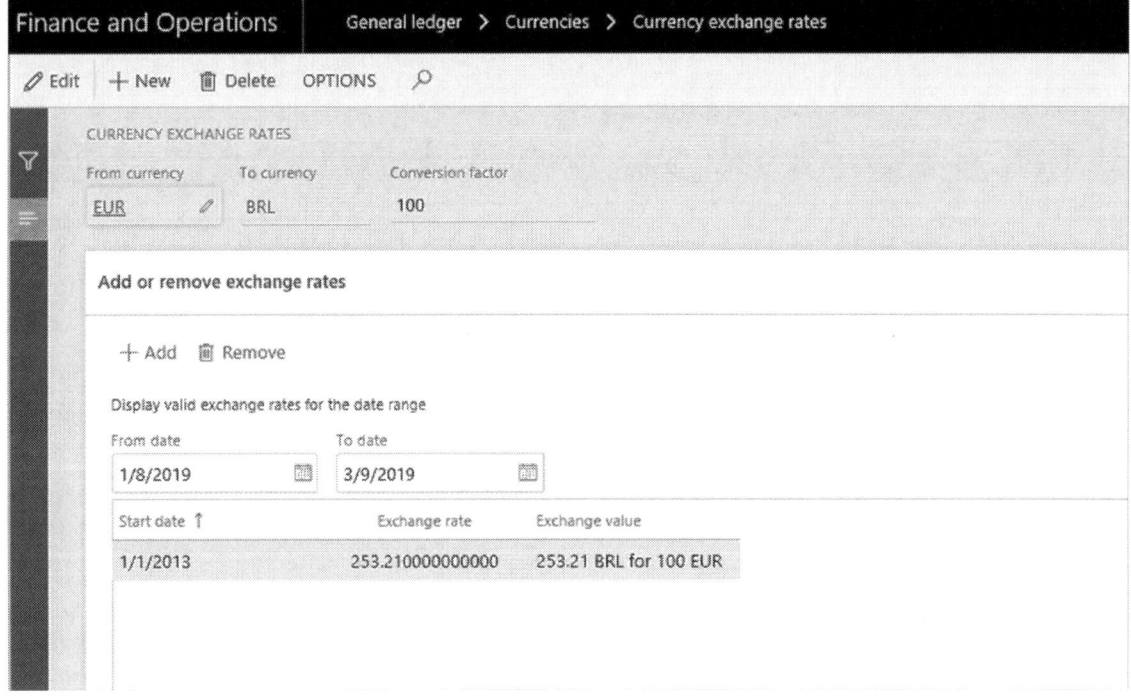

4.   If subsidiaries are associated with foreign currencies, from General Ledger open Accounts for automatic transactions
    1.   The 'Profit and loss account for consolidation differences' is for subsidiary companies that rely on a parent.
    2.   For a company that is financially independent of the parent choose 'Balance account for consolidation differences'.
        1.   In the main account field apply the account to be used for the currency adjustments.

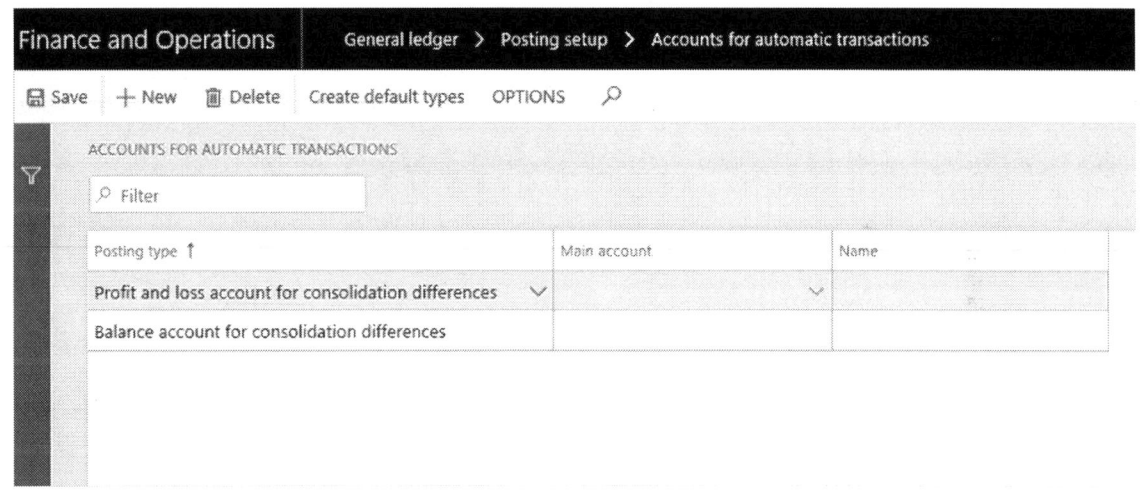

Currency Exchange Rates

1.   From General Ledger open the Currency exchange rates page
      1.   Select rate type

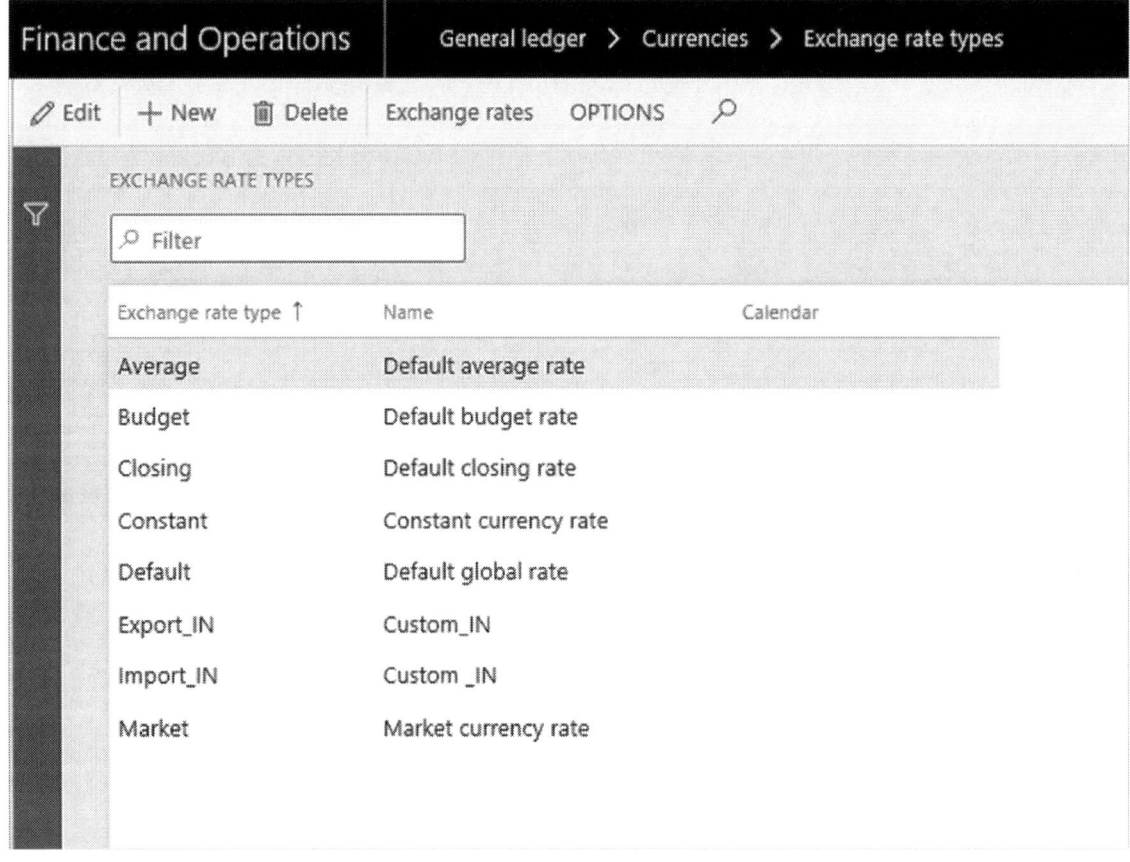

2. Open the Currency exchange rates page to determine currencies and setup rates

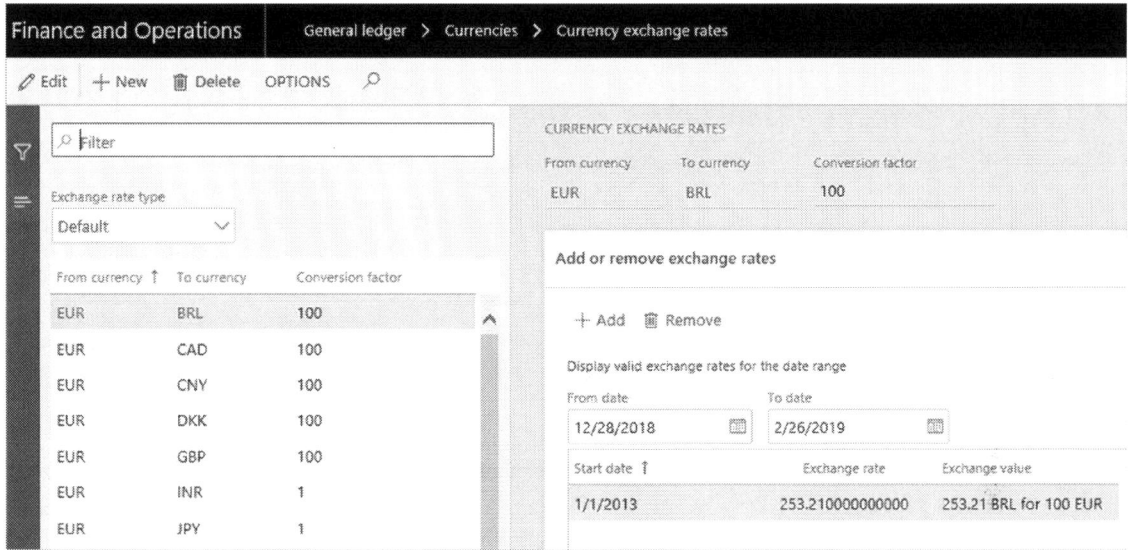

2. To enable import
1. From GL open Configure exchange rate providers

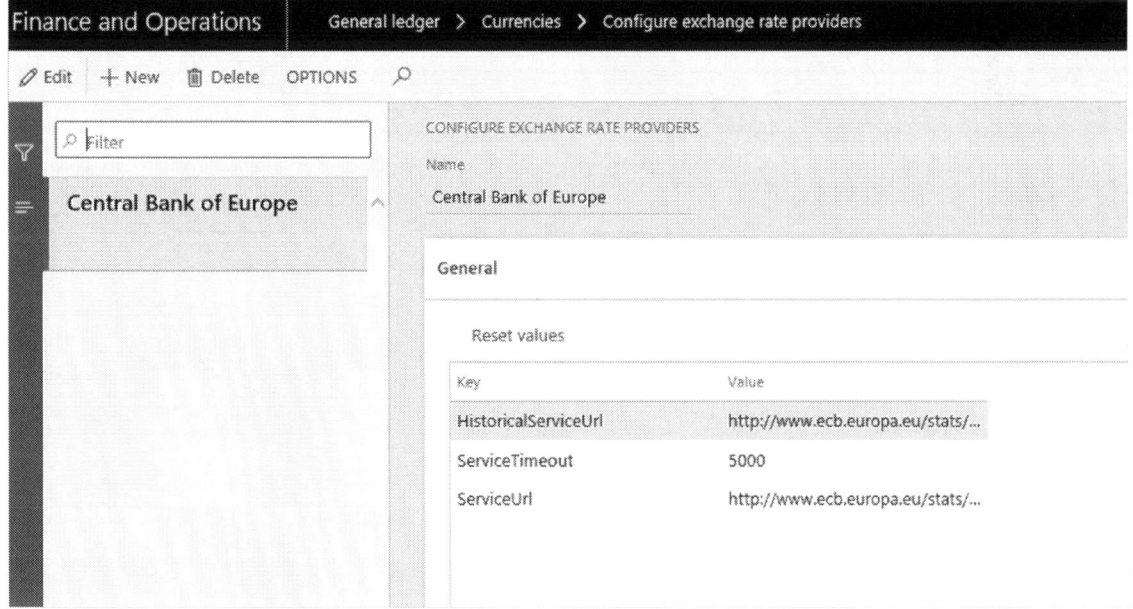

2. From GL open Import currency exchange rates

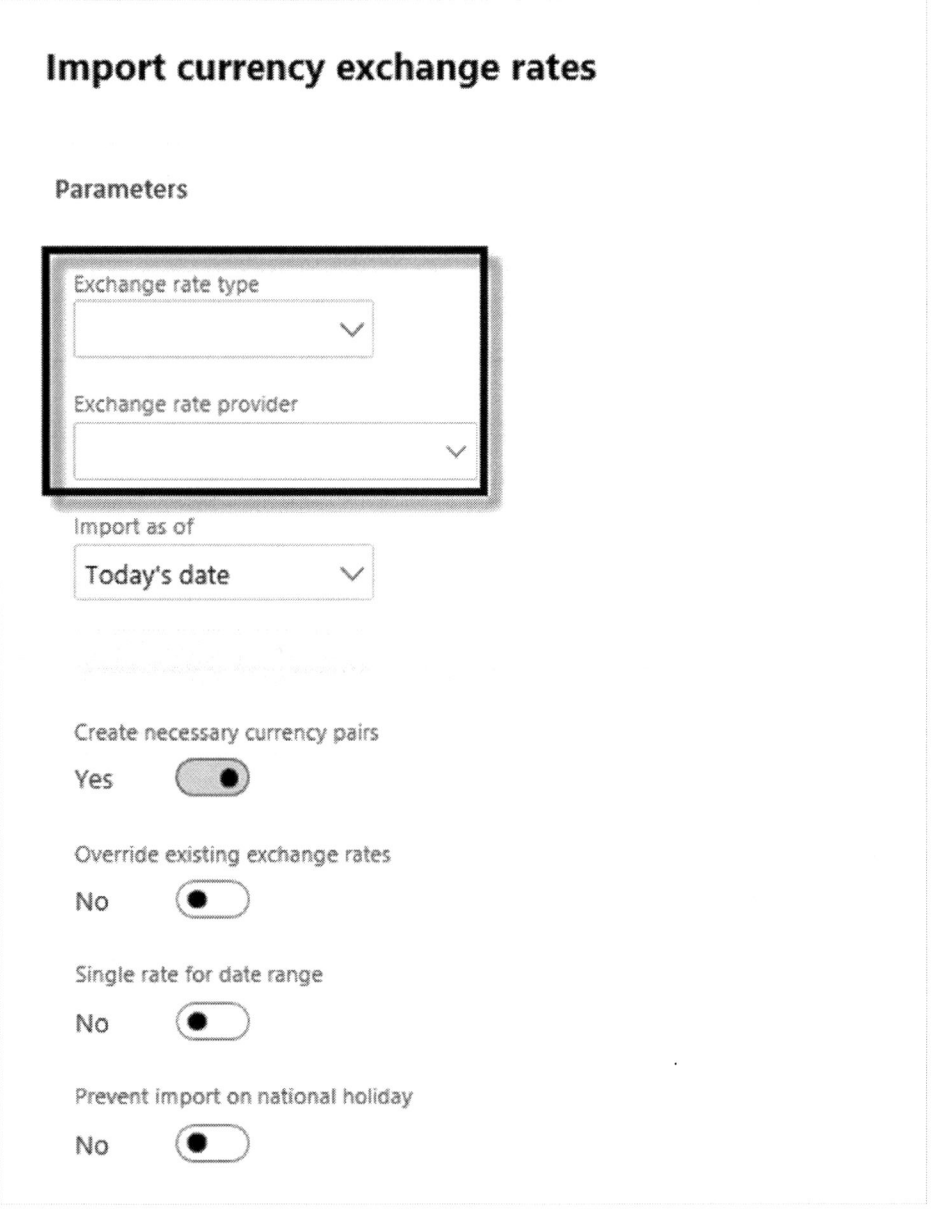

Import currency exchange rates

Parameters

Exchange rate type

Exchange rate provider

Import as of

Today's date

Create necessary currency pairs

Yes

Override existing exchange rates

No

Single rate for date range

No

Prevent import on national holiday

No

General Ledger Journal

1.   From General Ledger open General Ledger Journal
   1.   Click New and apply Name

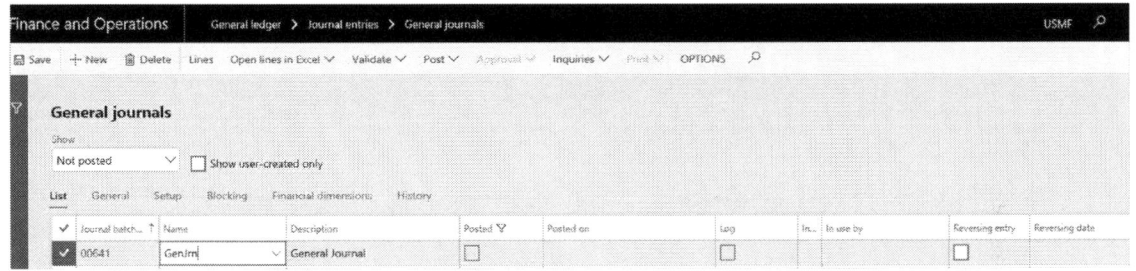

2.   From the Setup tab note account type

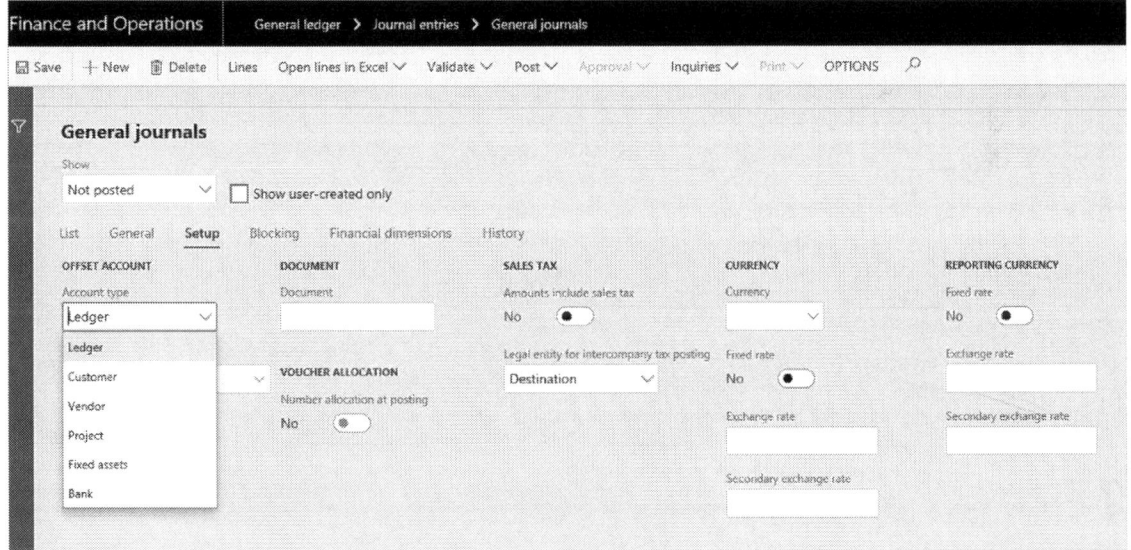

Main Accounts

1.   From General Ledger open Main Accounts
     1.   Input
          1.   Main account
          2.   Main account category
          3.   Db/Cr default
          4.   Currency
          5.   Currency translation type if applicable

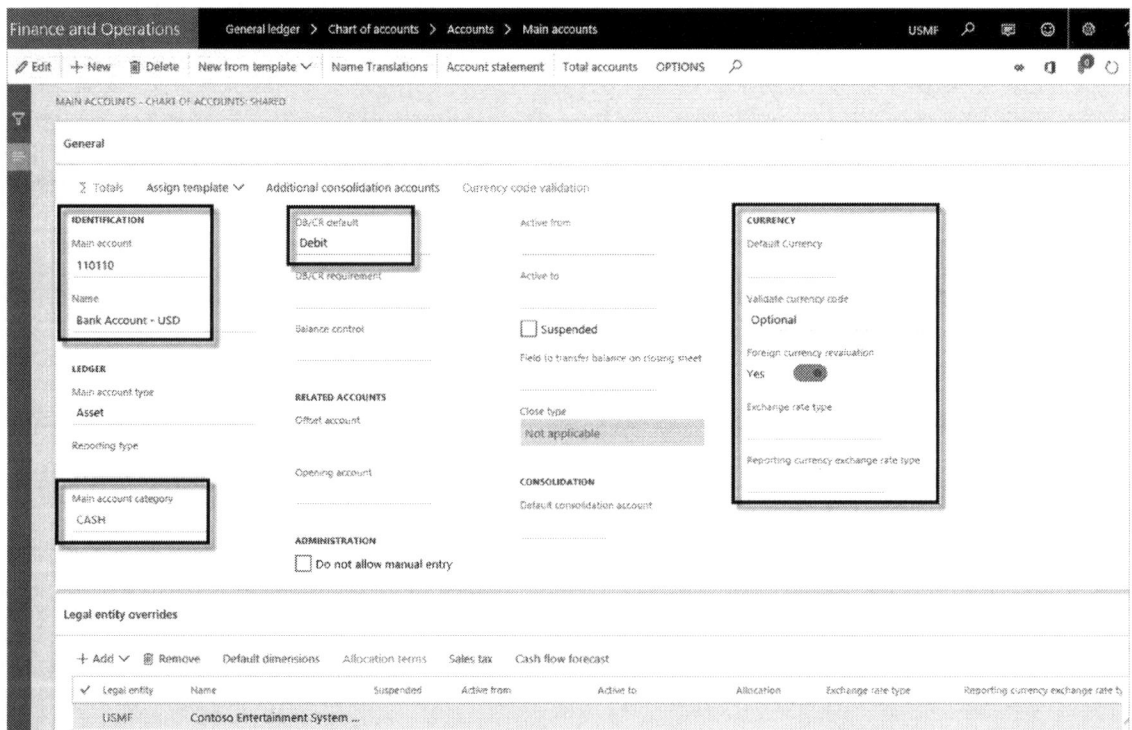

2. From General Ledger open Main Accounts Categories (see setup above on Main accounts)

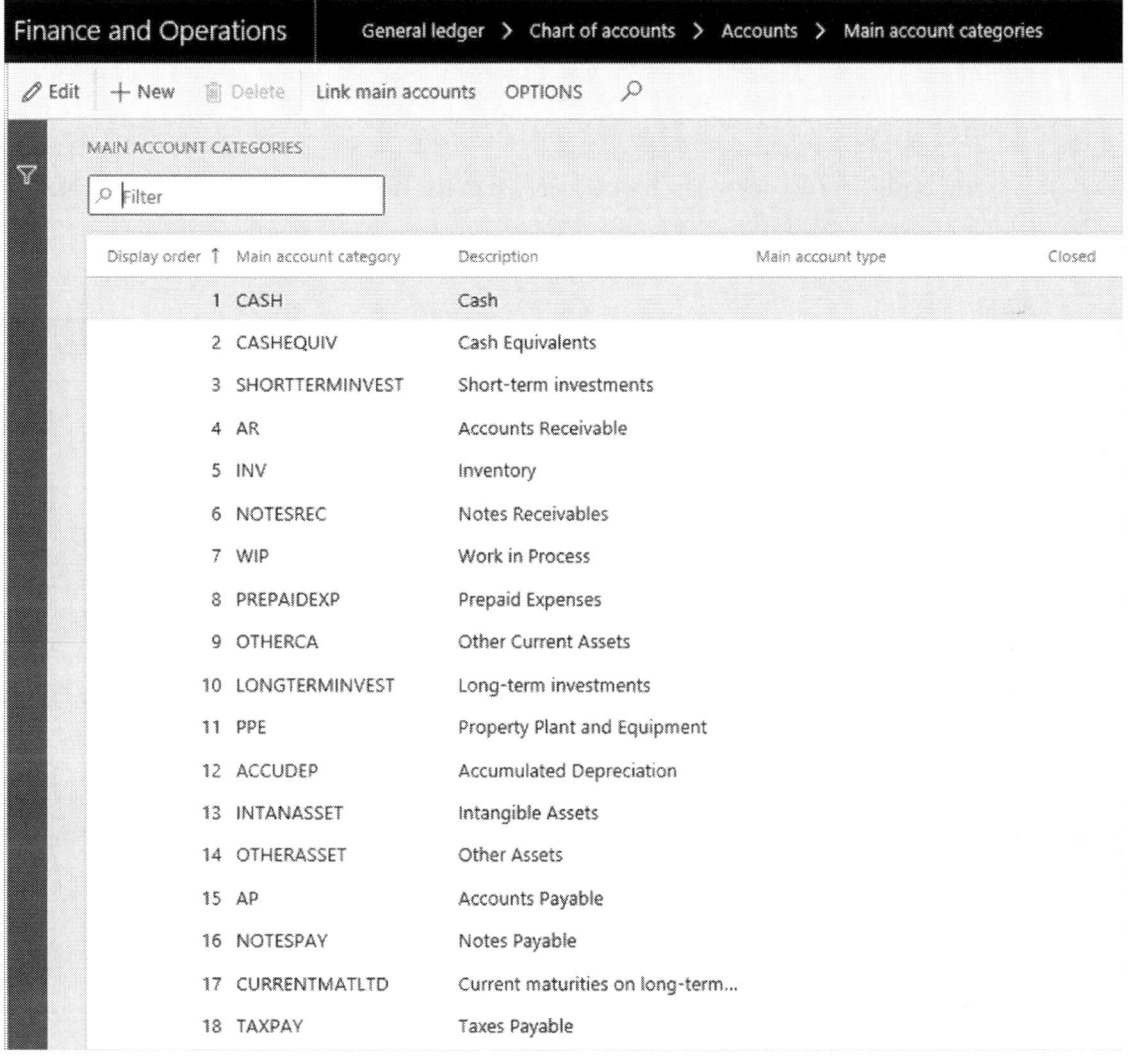

Fiscal Calendar

1.   From General Ledger open Fiscal calendar
    1.   Create before Ledger calendar
    2.   Operating periods record transactions
    3.   Note that calendars can be created for any length of time and that months and quarters are auto populated

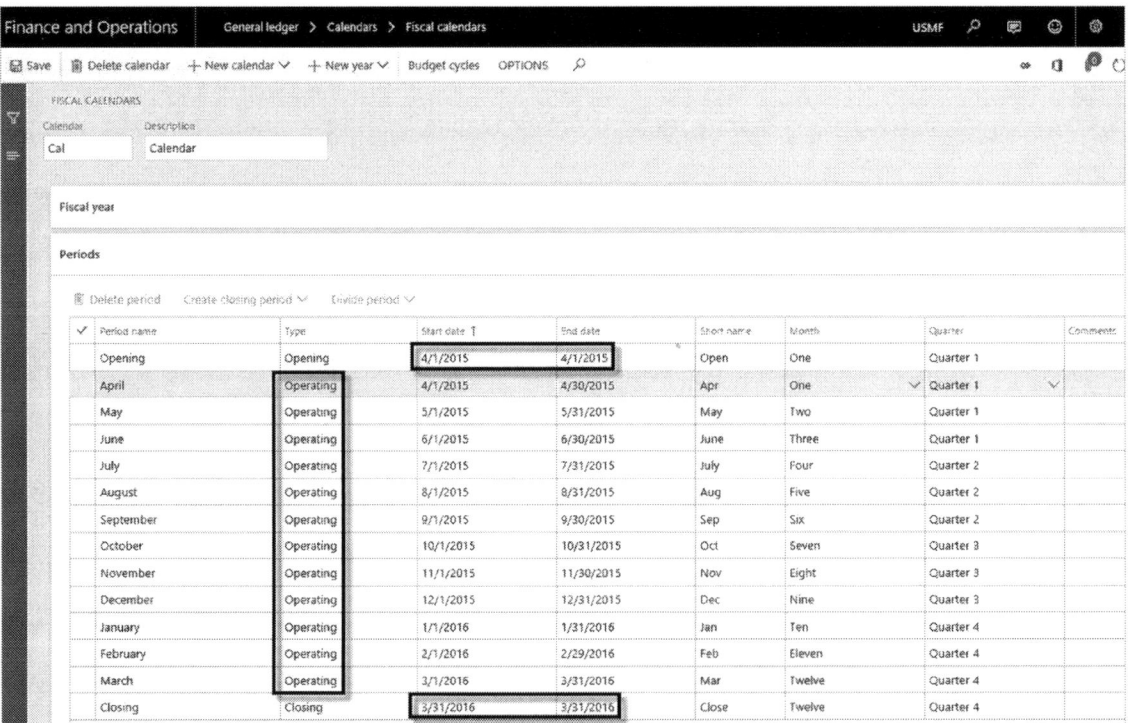

Financial Period Close Workspace

1. From Workspaces or from General Ledger open Financial Period Close Workspaces. Note MS docs: 'Financial Period Close Workspace' reference:

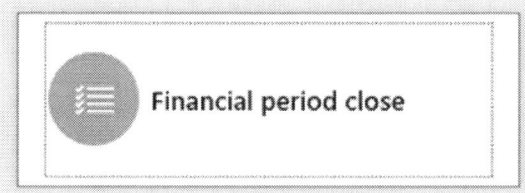

   1. View tasks by Past due, tasks remaining, tasks blocked or All Remaining
   2. Sort by fields on the grid
       1. Two indicators are used for tasks:
           1. An exclamation point icon indicates the task is past due
           2. A padlock icon indicates that the task depends on other tasks that not yet completed

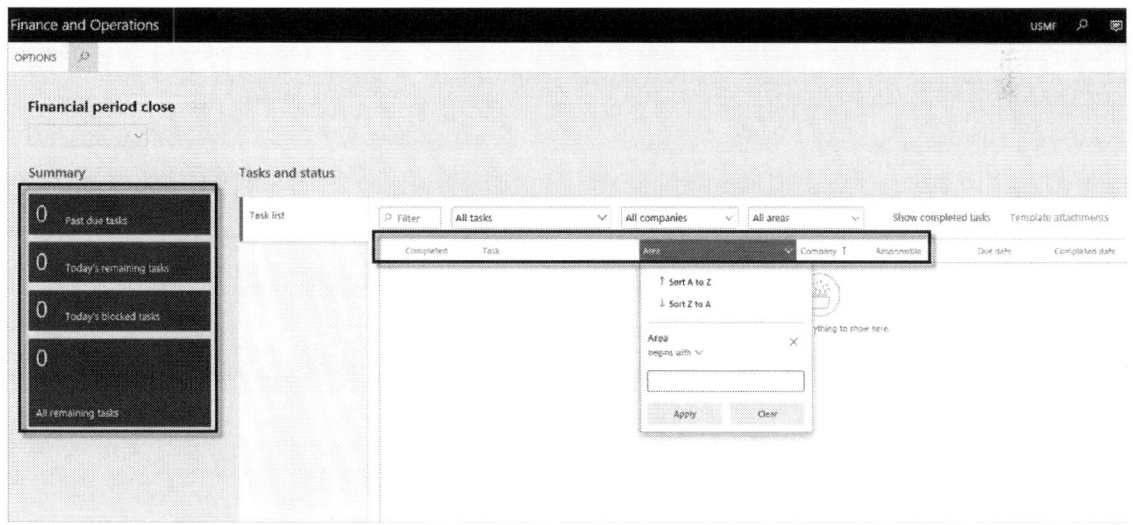

<u>Year End Closing</u>

1.   From GL open Main Account
    1.   See MS docs 'Year-end close' references:
    2.   Two types of transactions are created
        1.   Opening (always created)
        2.   Closing
    3.   Year-end closings are typically run multiple times
2.   Parameters
    1.   Delete close of year transactions
        1.   Voucher for previous end of year close is deleted, and a new voucher is created for all accounts for beginning balances
    2.   Closing transactions require the create closing transactions check button enabled to Yes
        1.   Is used to bring the balances of the profit and loss accounts to zero
    3.   Set fiscal year status to permanently closed
        1.   If set to yes the prior period is permanently closed. Best practice, place the period Hold, using a setting of No
    4.   Voucher number must be filled in parameter
        1.   Set to yes. Opening transactions will have a voucher associated with them.

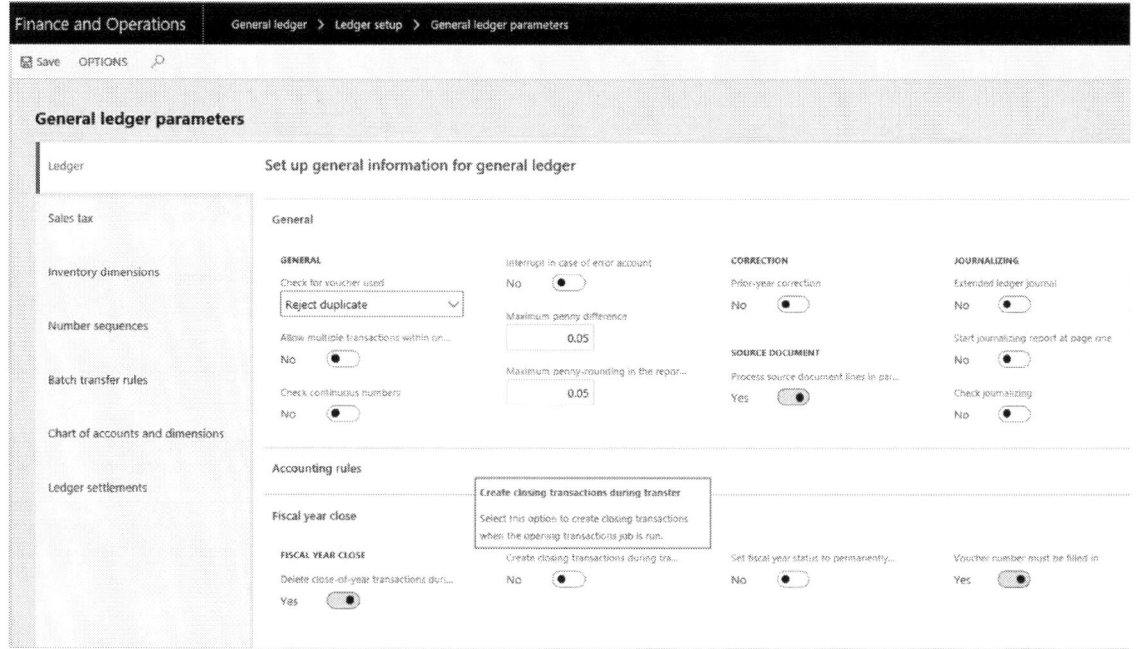

3. Create next fiscal calendar
4. Put prior periods on hold in ledger colanders
5. From GL open Year End Close (note that this process is different from AX 12)
   1. Update entities and/or dimensions
      1. If dimensions are set to no, will transfer by the ledger account only
         1. Note that dimensions can be closed all, or at single if dimensions are not to be rolled forward to the main account

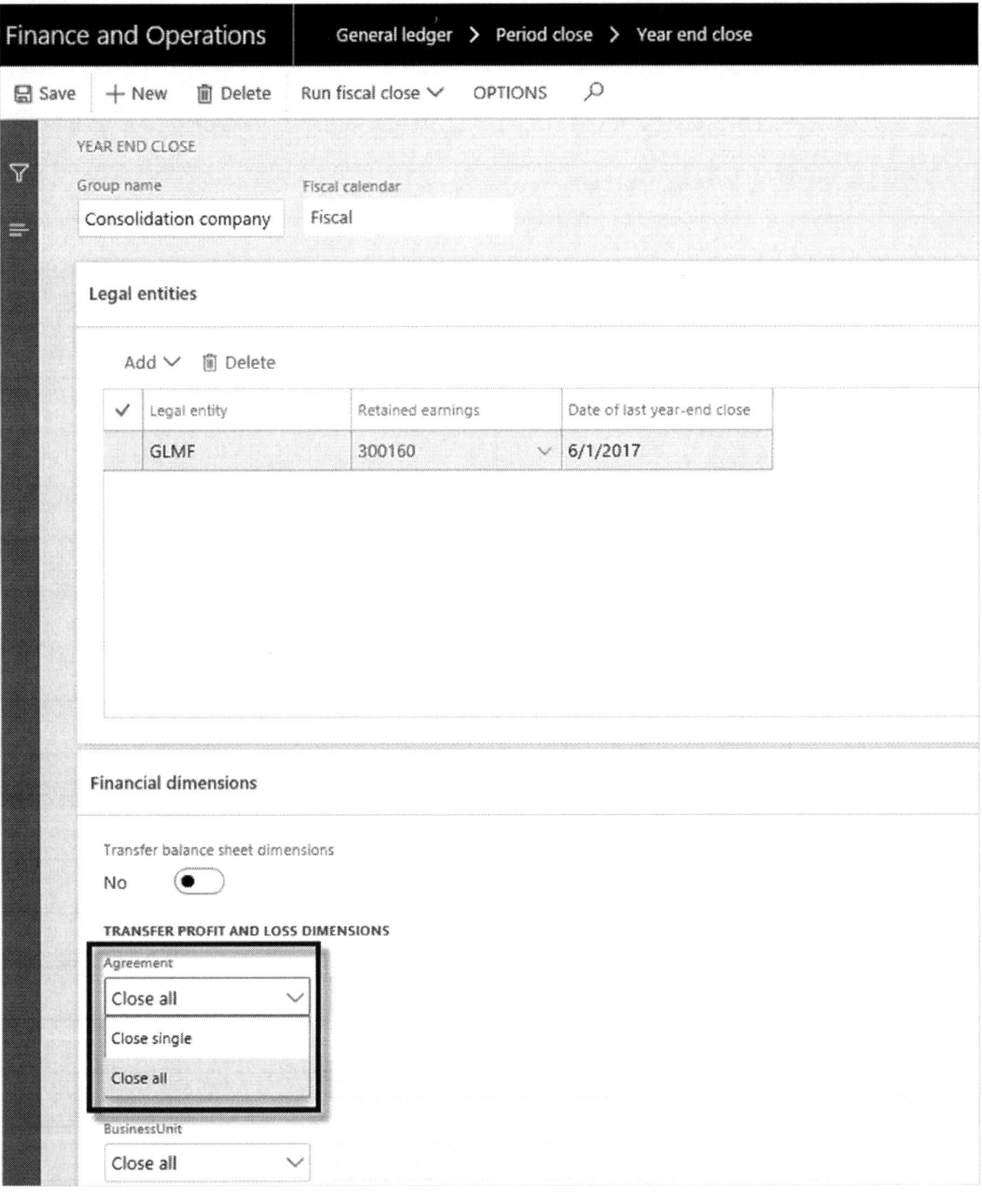

2. Click run fiscal close
    1. Select year and input voucher (batch is recommended)

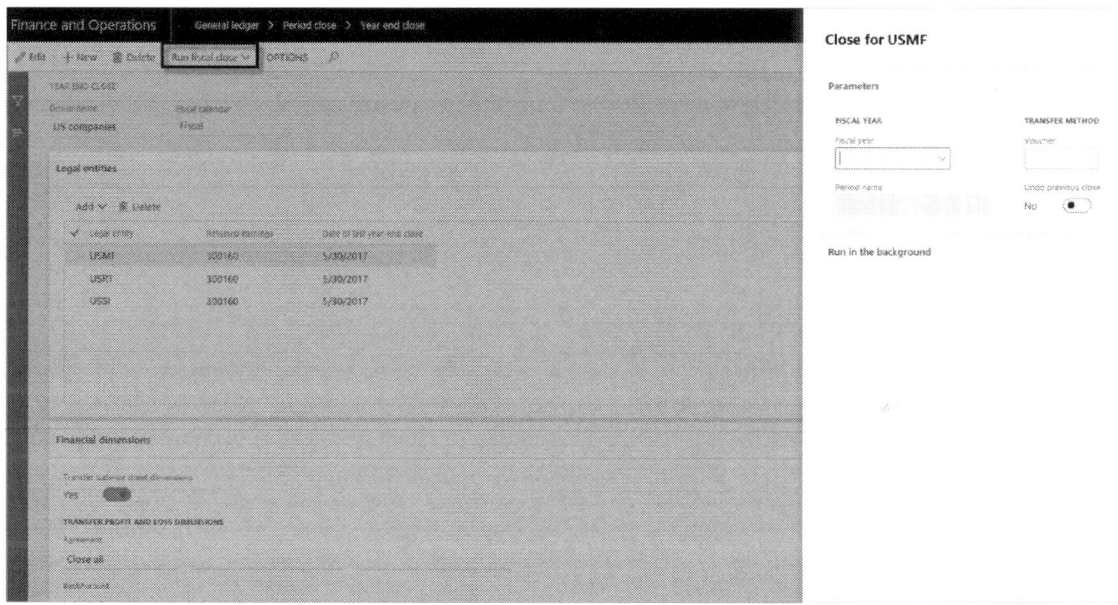

6.   When complete open Trial Balance

1.   Opening voucher balances can be viewed from hyperlink on field

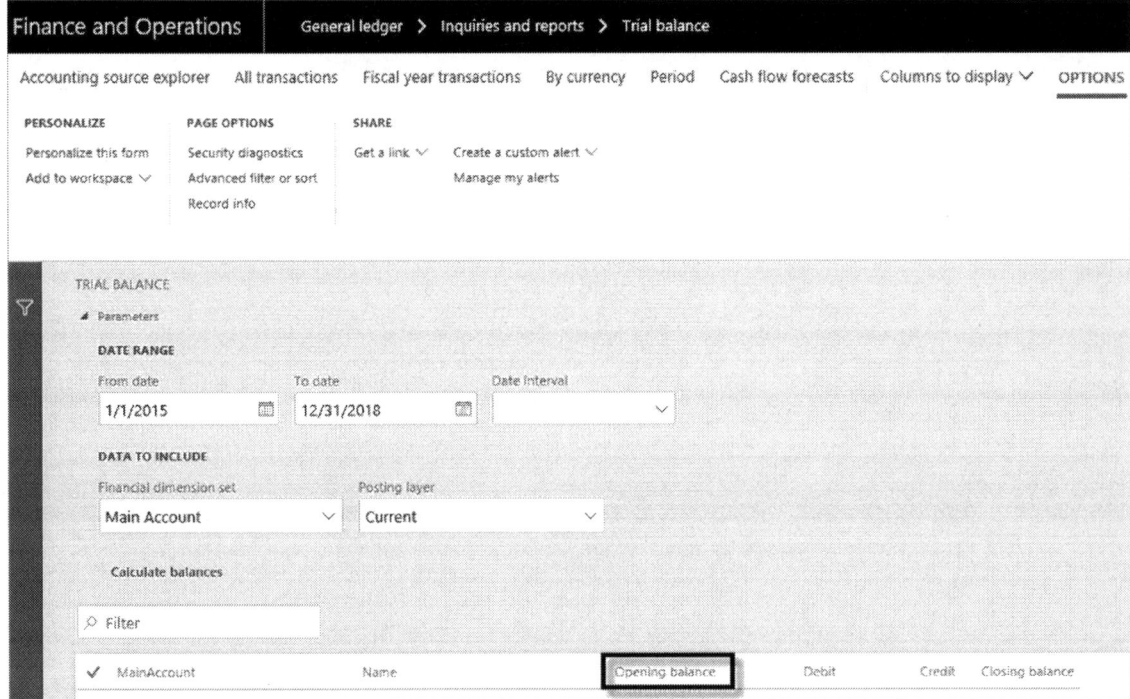

Main Account Allocations

1. From GL open Main Accounts
    1. If Allocation is required click on Allocation, and click Allocation Terms
        1. Note, allocation basis is used with allocation rules

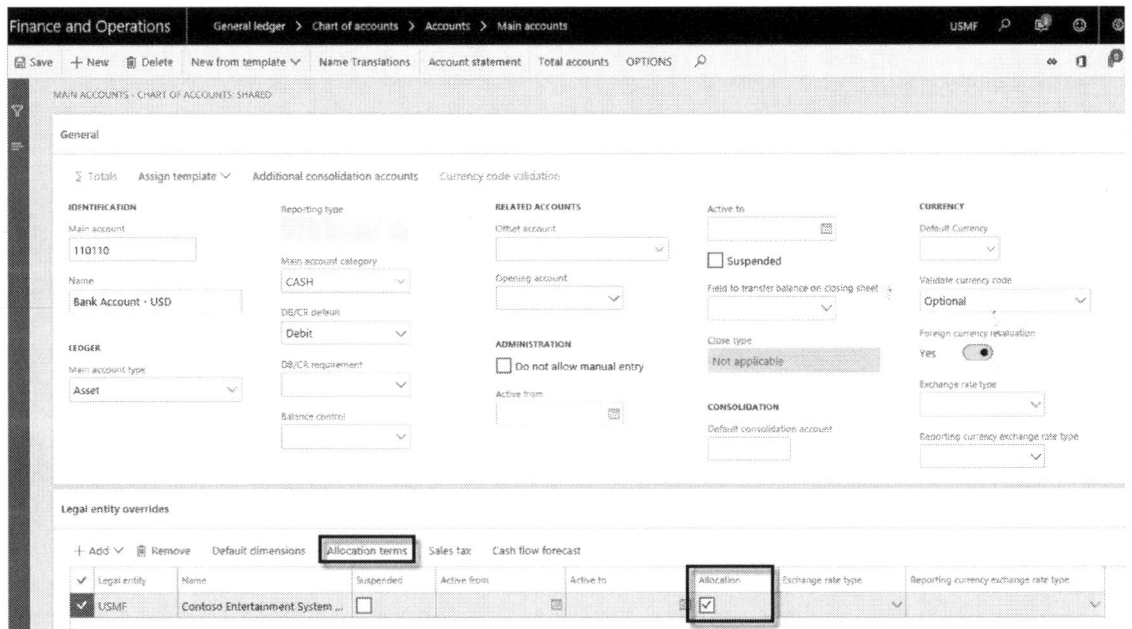

2.   Apply percent and setup criteria

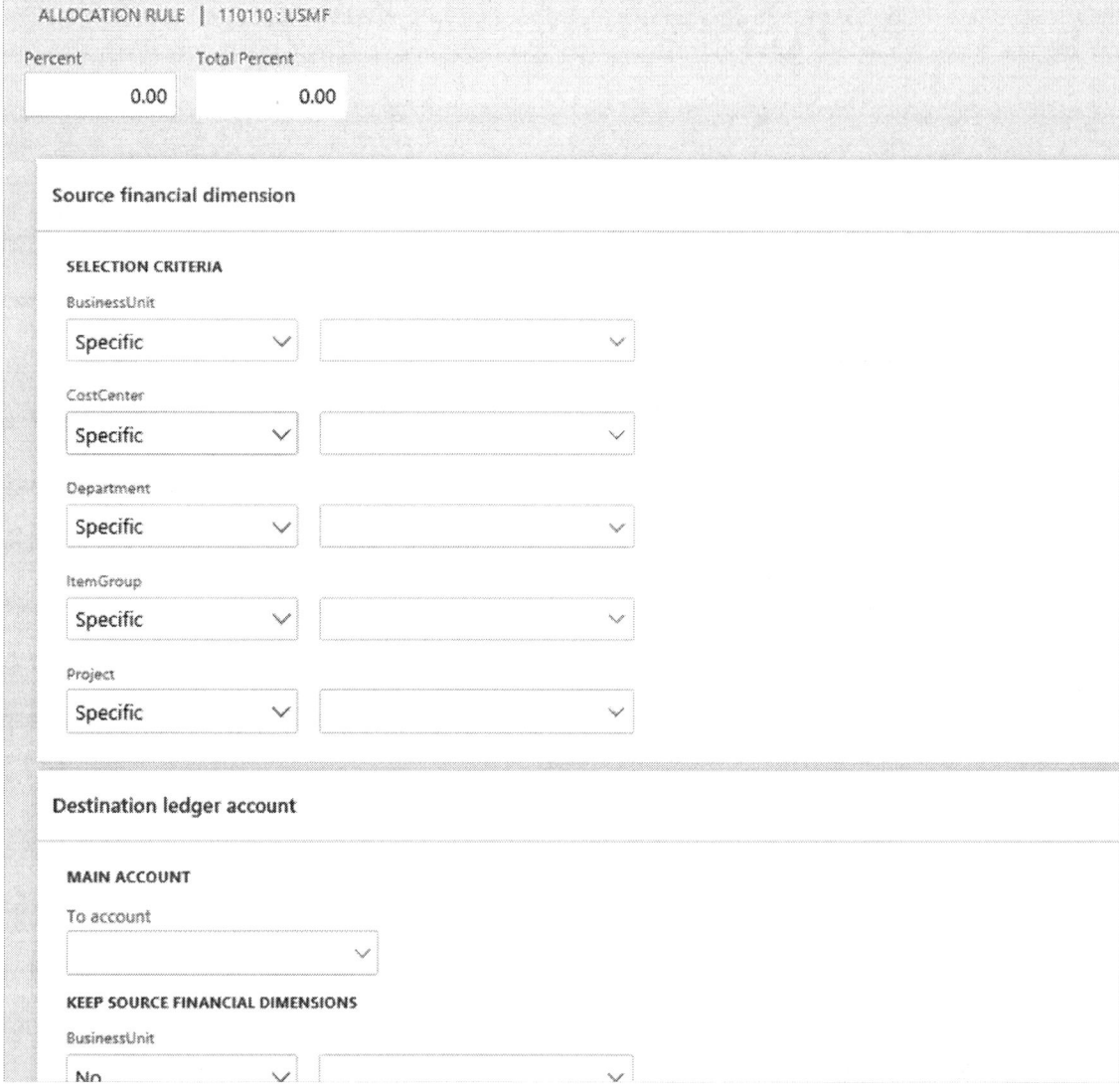

3.   To allocate based on actual ledger balances for a variable combination of accounts or dimensions, the basis method for rules must be used. See MS docs: 'Ledger Allocation Rules' reference:

    1.   An allocation rule has several components

        1.   The source: select the accounts and dimensions to use for the allocation. The total of the amount will constitute the base of the allocation.

        2.   The destination: select all the combinations of account and dimensions that will receive an amount.

        3.   The rule: select the calculation type of the allocation. It can be fixed (a percentage) or variable (linked to another account)

    2.   If variable, setup Ledger Allocation Basis

        1.   Click New and input basis ID

        2.   Click Source

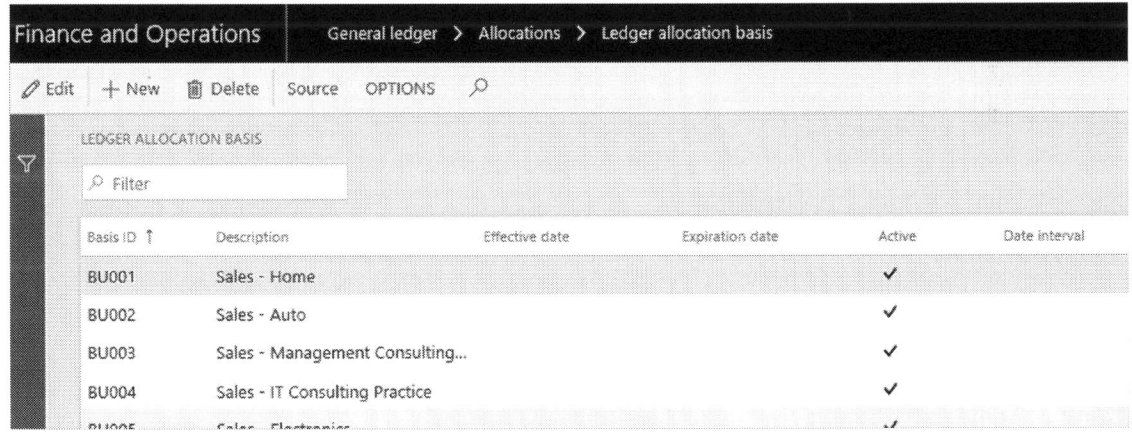

3. Click New and input source account and dimension

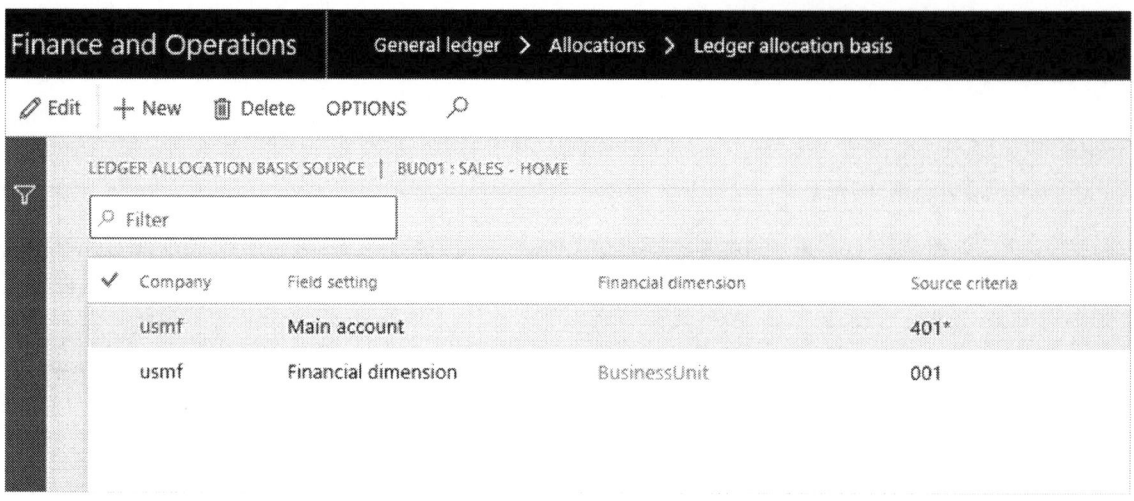

4. Repeat for additional basis allocations
5. Create Ledger Allocation Rules

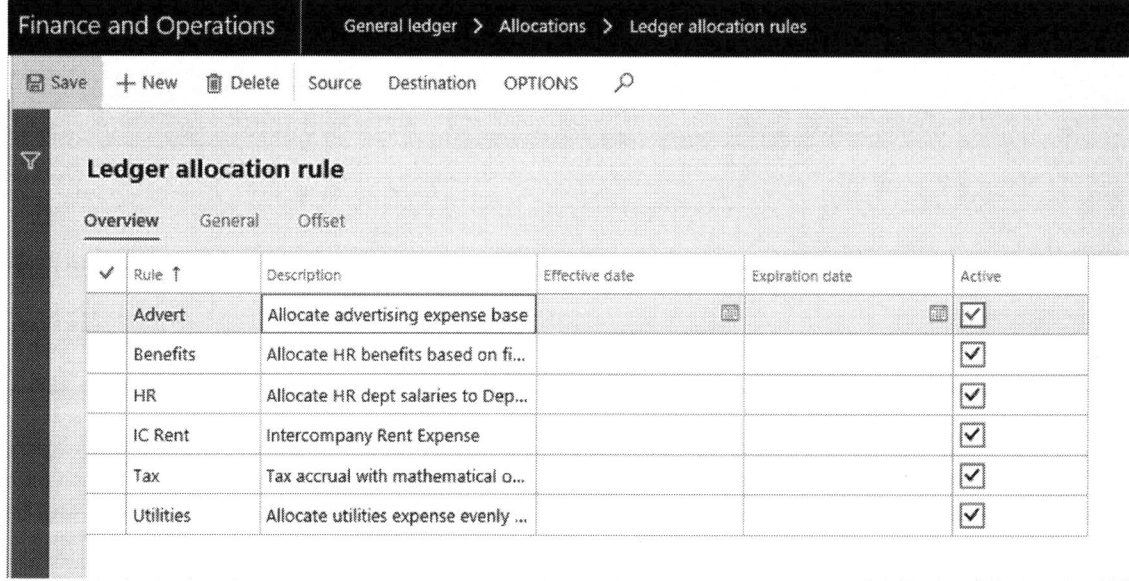

1.   Note allocation method and journal on General tab
2.   Click the Offset tab

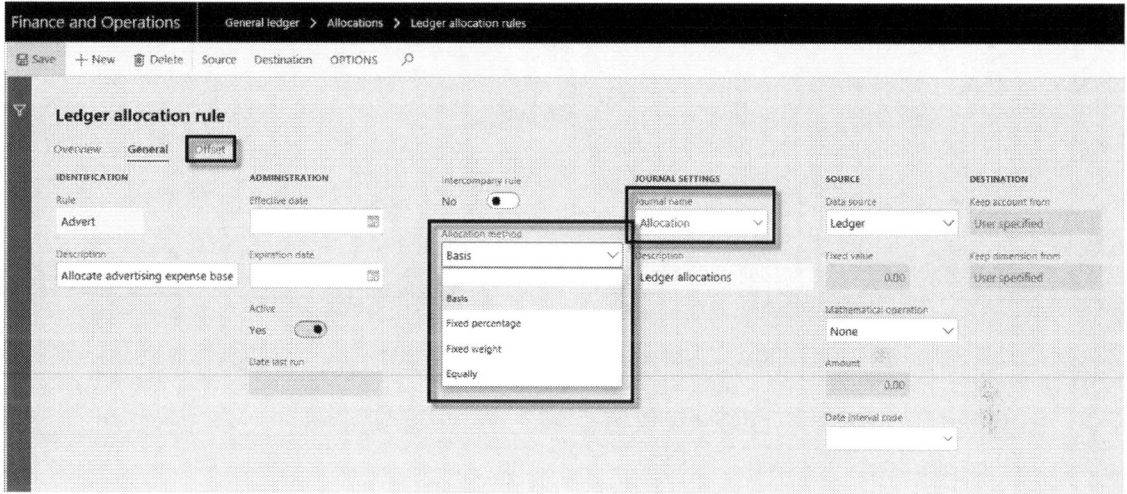

3. Select the offset account
   1. In this example the credit will be applied to the same account used in the source in order to have a zero balance after the allocation.
   2. Click the Source button

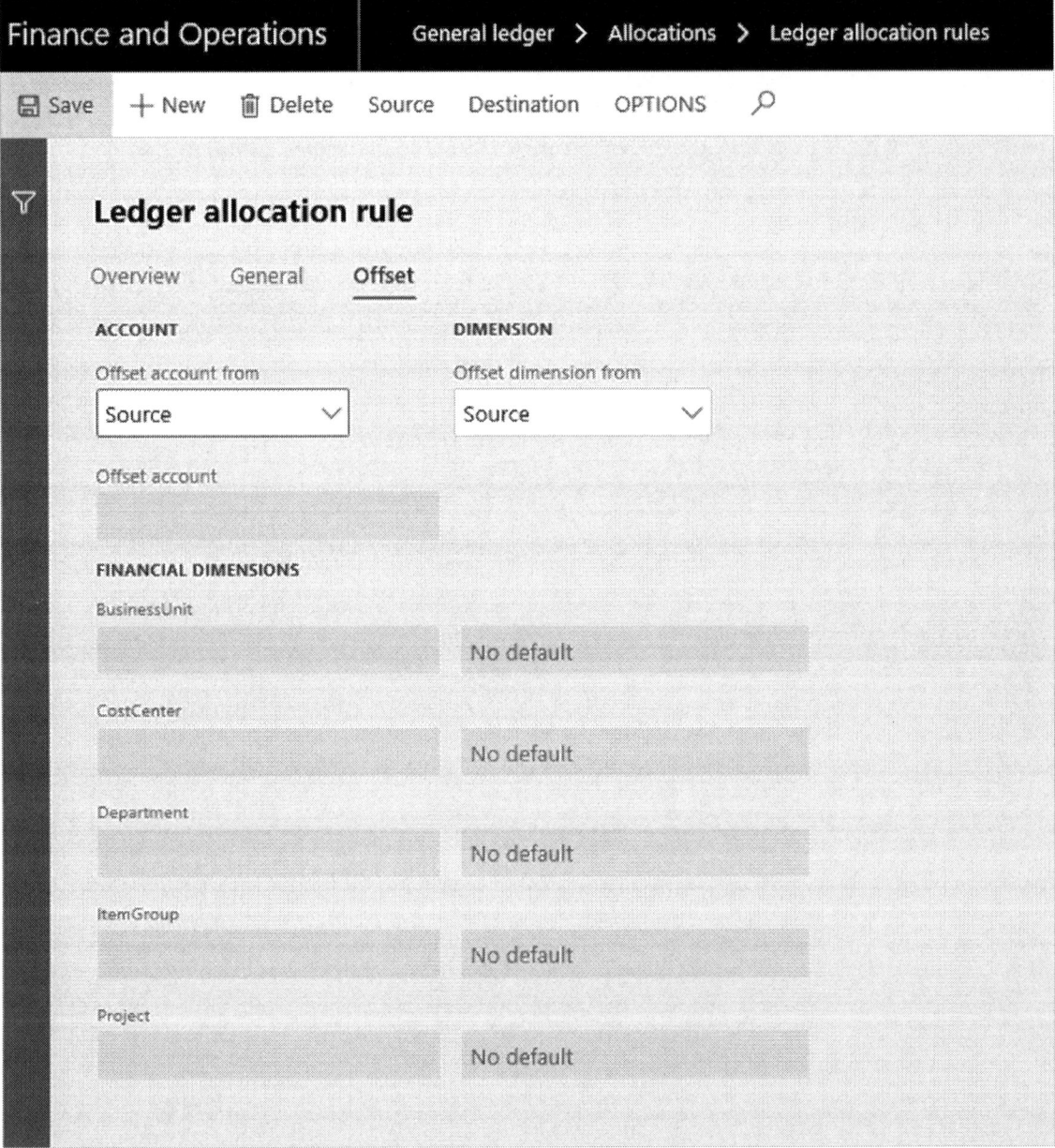

4.   Select the offset account
   1.   Select the relevant main account and if required add a dimension via New
   2.   Click the Destination button

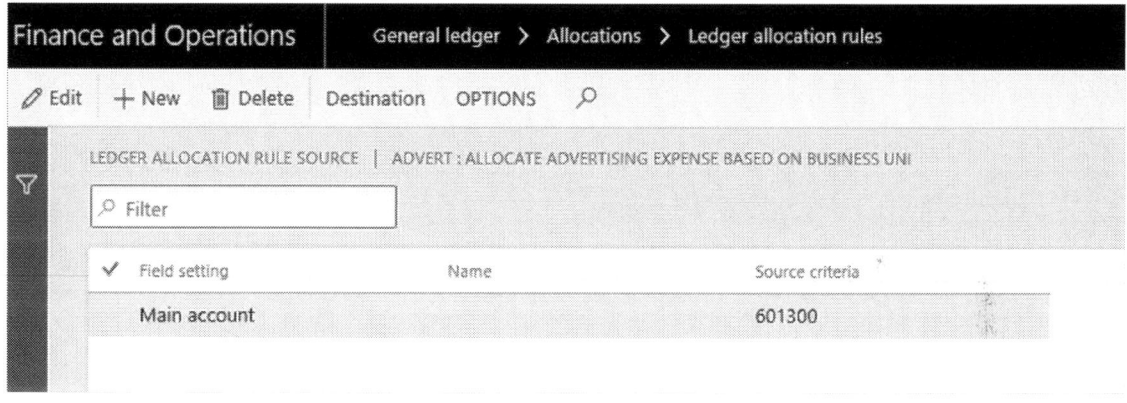

5.   Create lines with the basis rule(s)

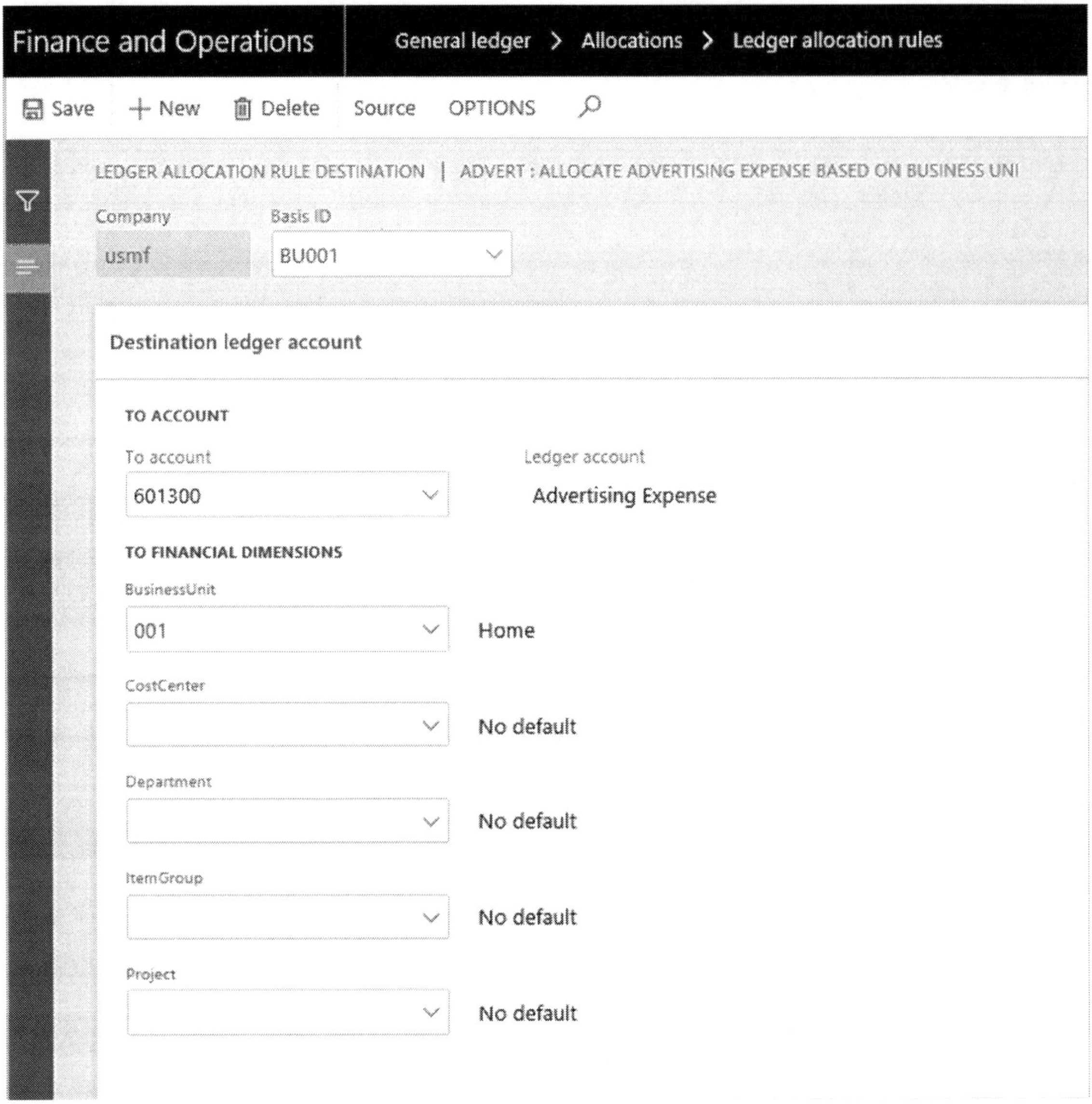

🖫 Save   + New   🗑 Delete   Source   OPTIONS   🔎

LEDGER ALLOCATION RULE DESTINATION | ADVERT : ALLOCATE ADVERTISING EXPENSE BASED ON BUSINESS UNI

Company   Basis ID

usmf   BU001   ∨

Destination ledger account

TO ACCOUNT

To account   Ledger account

601300   ∨   Advertising Expense

TO FINANCIAL DIMENSIONS

BusinessUnit

001   ∨   Home

CostCenter

                            ∨   No default

Department

                            ∨   No default

ItemGroup

                            ∨   No default

Project

                            ∨   No default

6.   Activate the rule

Active
✓

Ledger Allocation Rules

1.   From GL open Ledger allocation rules
      1.   See MS docs: 'Ledger allocation rules'

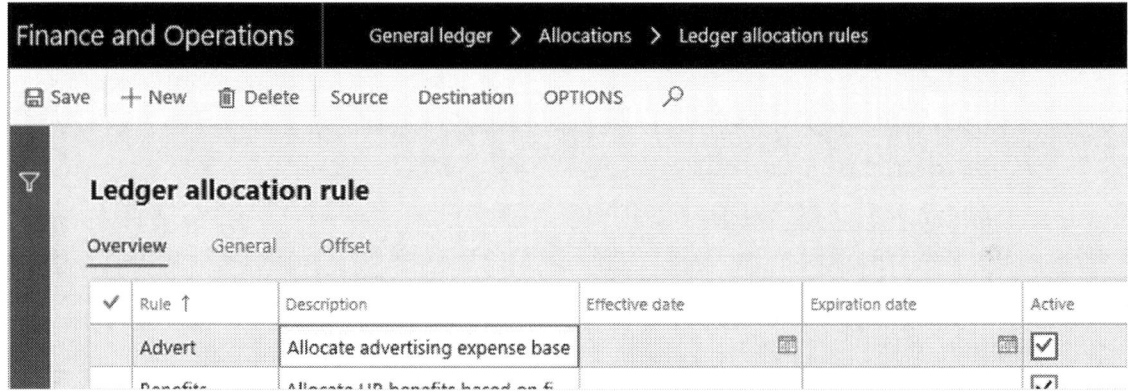

2.   Click General tab, note allocation method

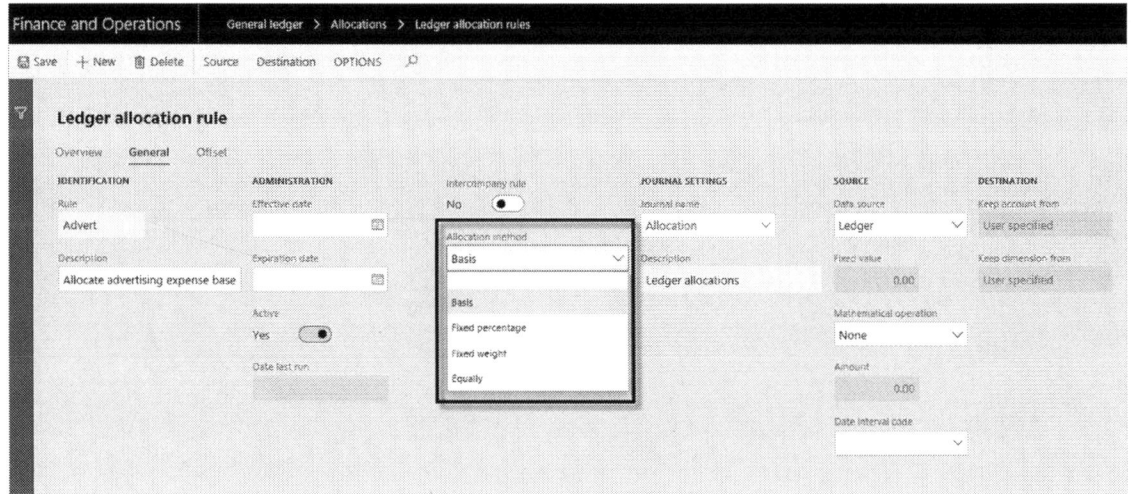

Setup Centralized Payments

1. See MS docs 'Set up centralized payments'
2. **Note form paths on screen copies**
3. From <u>Organization Administration</u> open Organization hierarchies
   1. Is used for both customer and vendor centralized payments

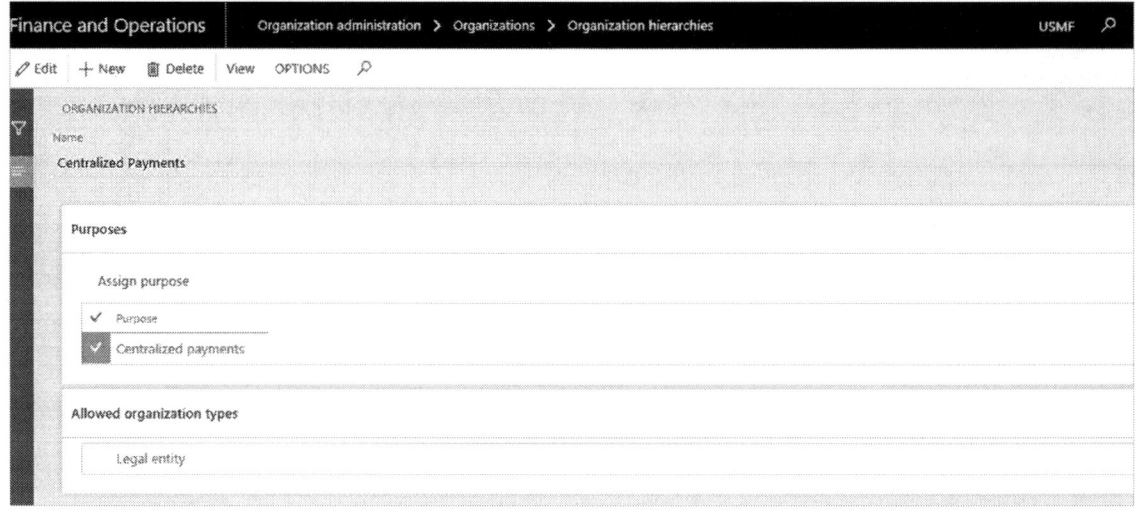

4.   From <u>GL</u> open Intercompany accounting
   1.   Due to and Due from transaction creation for legal entities
        (originating and destination)

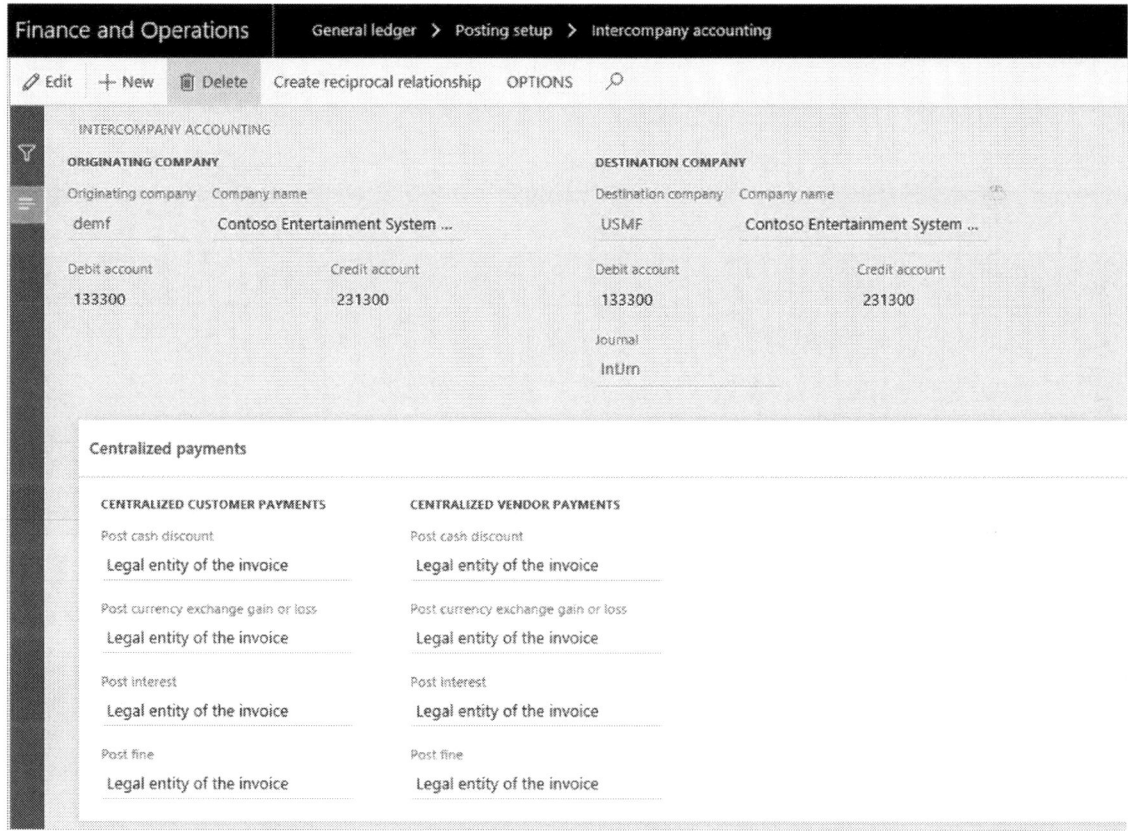

5.   From <u>AP</u> open All vendors
6.   Map vendor accounts
       1.   Same address book setup for vendor pays and customer accounts
       2.   Vendor account example

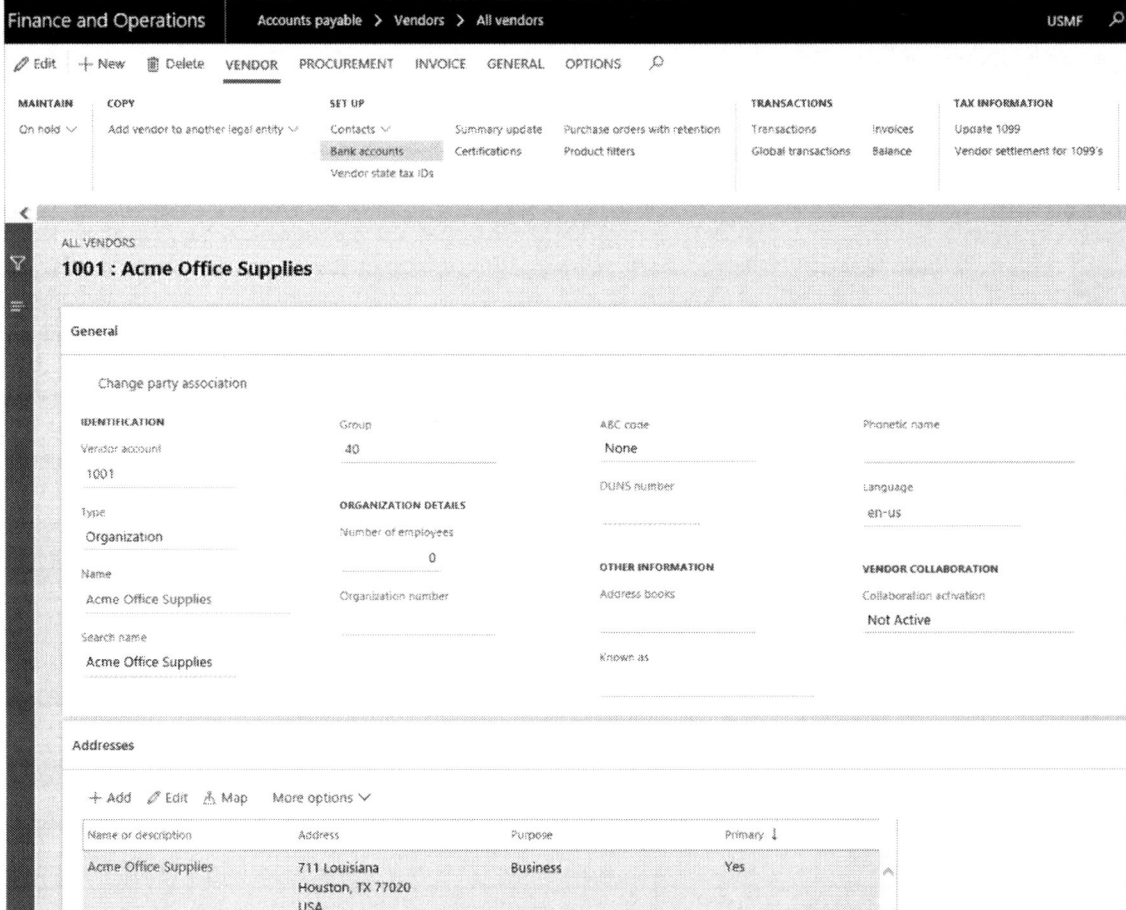

7.   From <u>AP</u> open Vendor posting profiles

8.   Centralized posting profiles

      1.   Posting profile ID's must be the same in each legal entity for processing payments

      2.   Note MS docs 'Set up centralized payments' reference: The selections that you make for the posting profile in the legal entity of the invoice don't have to match the setup of the posting profile in the legal entity of the payment.

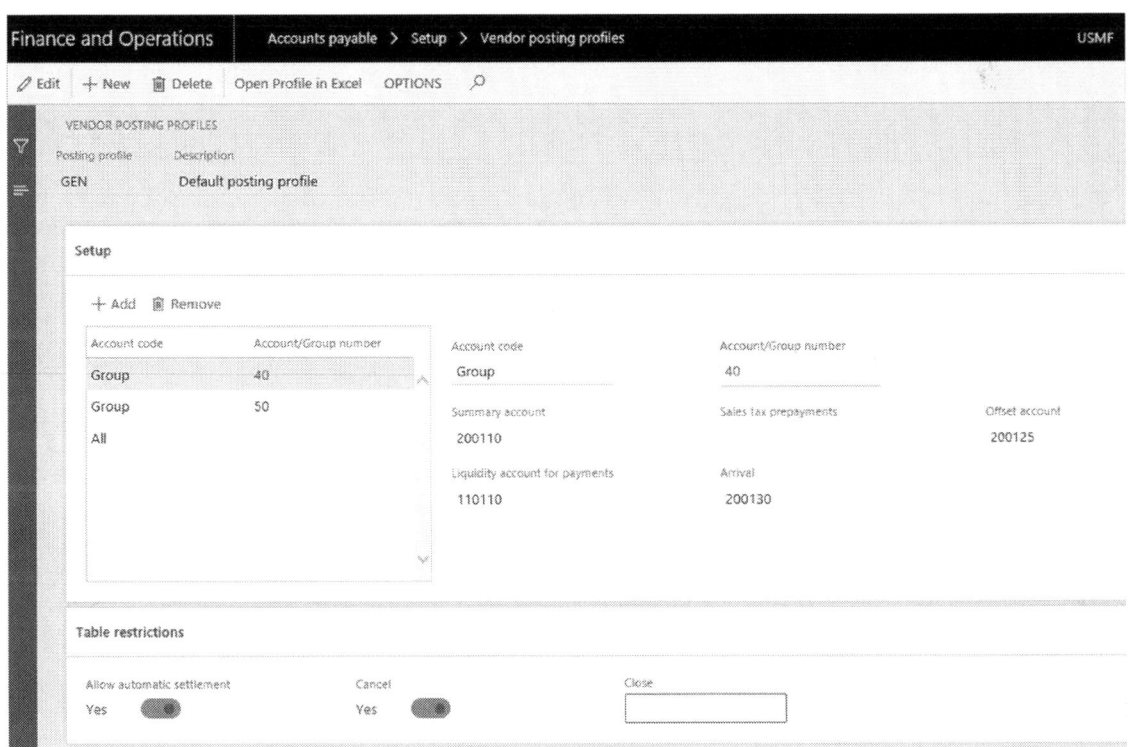

9. From <u>AP</u> open Methods of Payment
10. Centralized methods of payment
    1. Method of payment ID's must match
    2. Note MS doc reference: The selections that you make for the method of payment in the legal entity of the invoice don't have to match the setup of the method of payment in the legal entity of the payment.

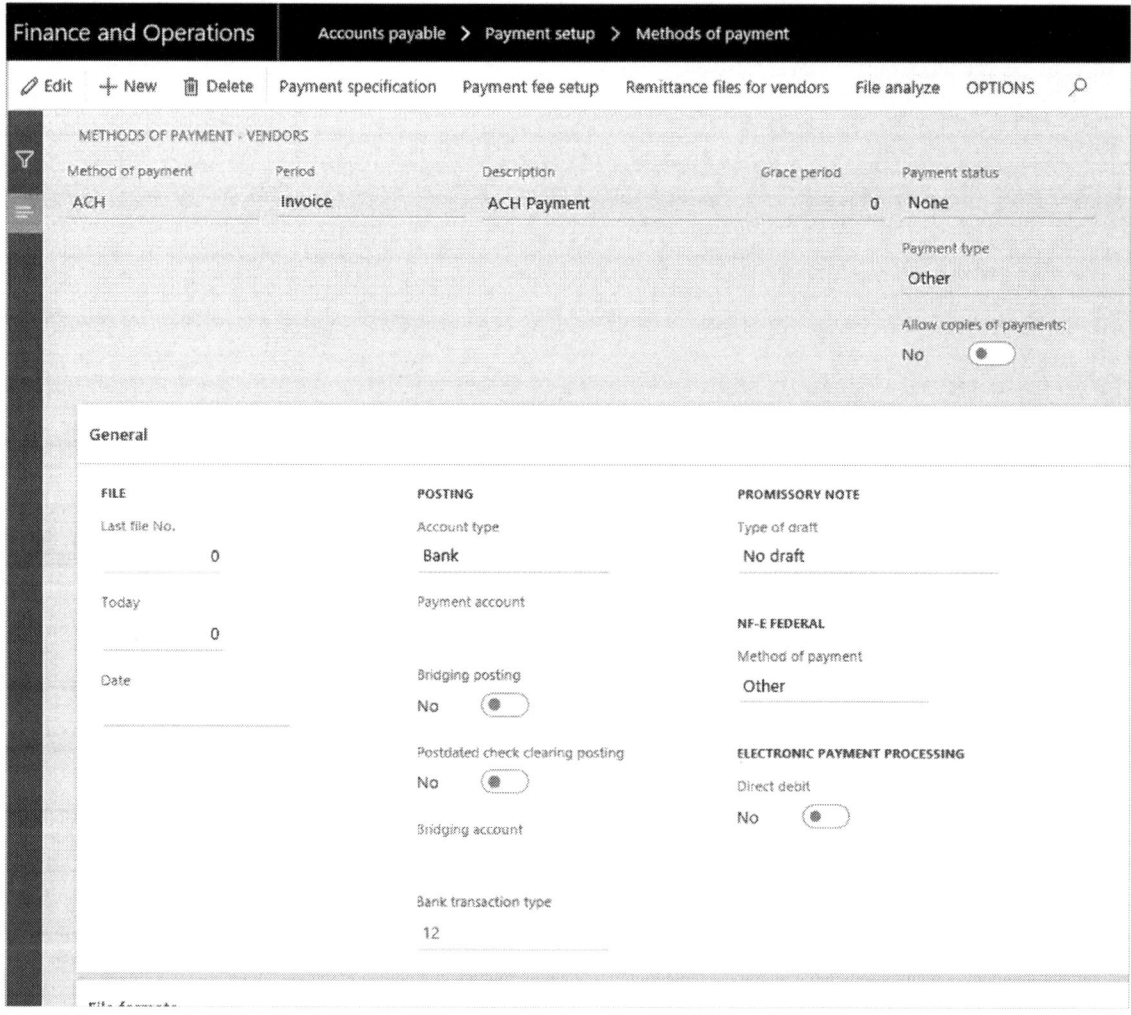

11. From <u>GL</u> open Default descriptions
    1. Is included in Due to and Due from transactions
    2. For Intercompany customer settlement and Intercompany vendor settlement

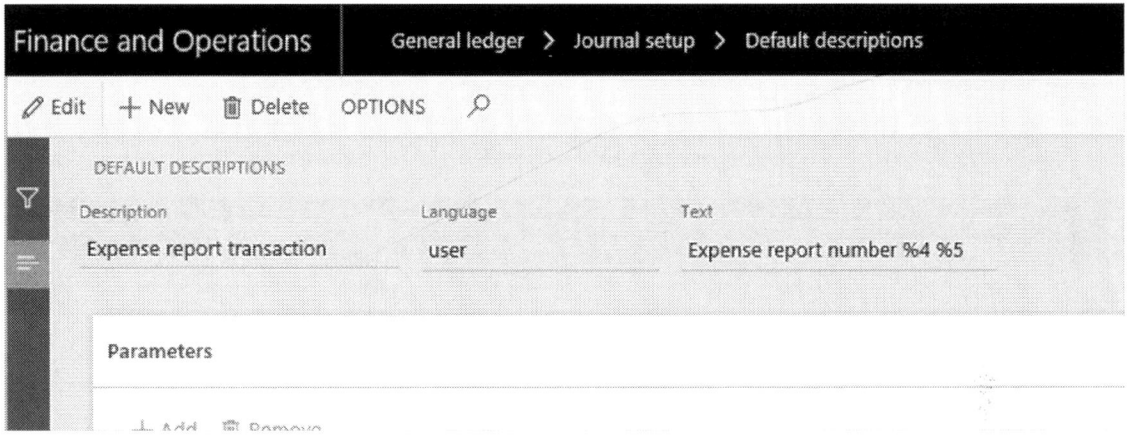

Account for Automatic Transactions

1. From GL open Accounts for automatic transactions
    1. The first time an automatic transaction is set up the Default Type button is available for selection

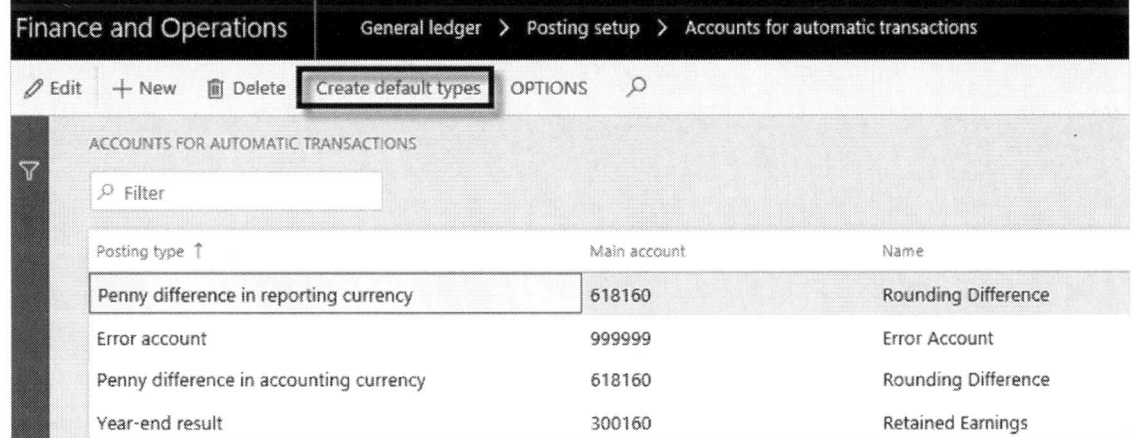

FIXED ASSETS

Disposal of Fixed Asset

1.   From Fixed Assets open the Fixed Assets Journal

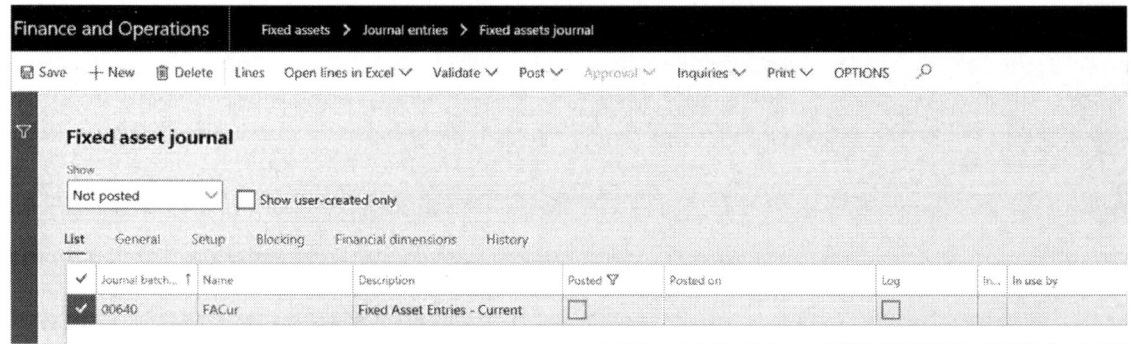

2.   Click Lines, and assign type, disposal

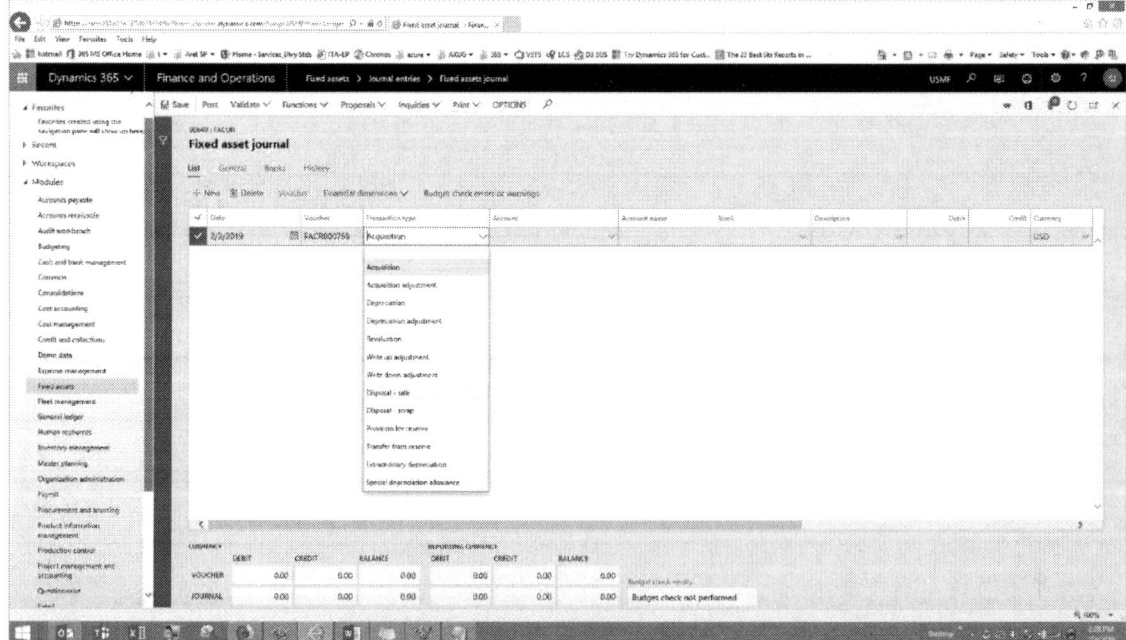

Fixed Asset Journal Acquisition

Proposal

1.   Note, FA acquisition methods also include
    1.   GL, manual
    2.   Vendor invoice journal, manual
    3.   PO, automatic
2.   From Fixed Assets open Fixed Assets Journals
    1.   Click New

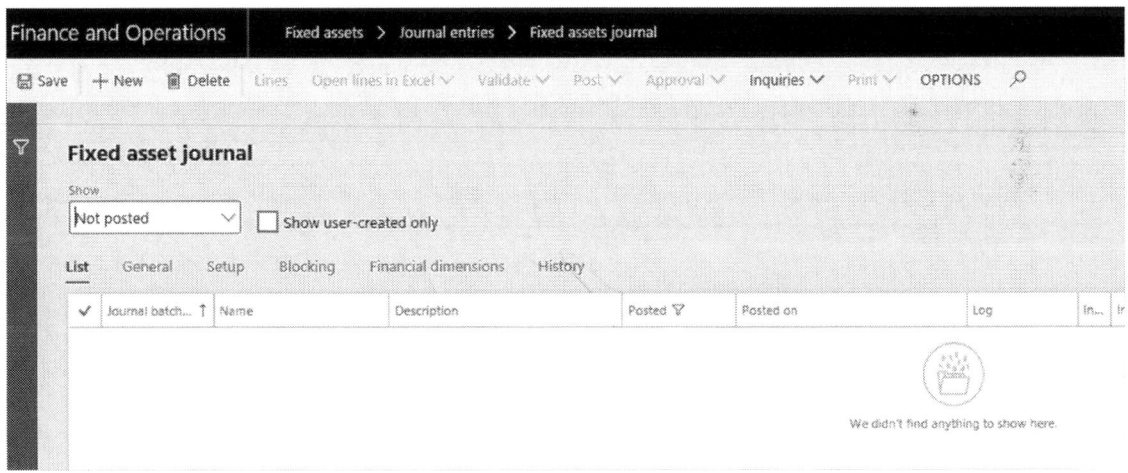

3.   Click Lines

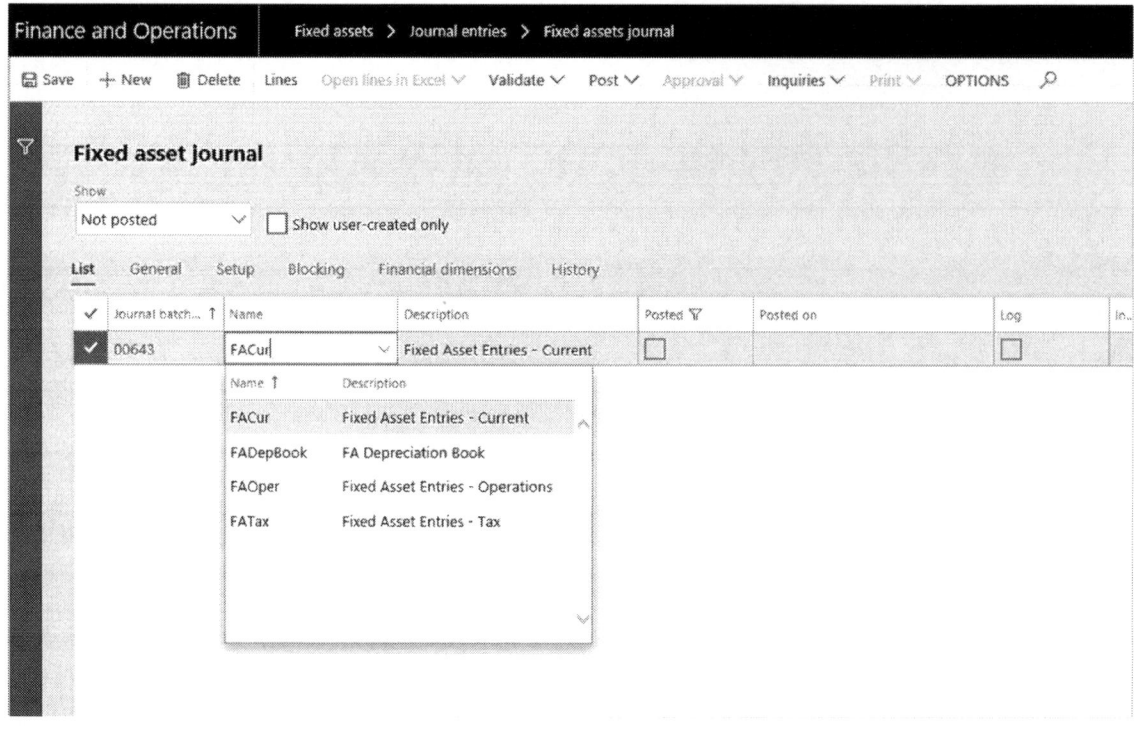

4.   Click the Proposals drop down and select Acquisition Proposal
    1.   Pop up allows for filtered selections
    2.   Click OK

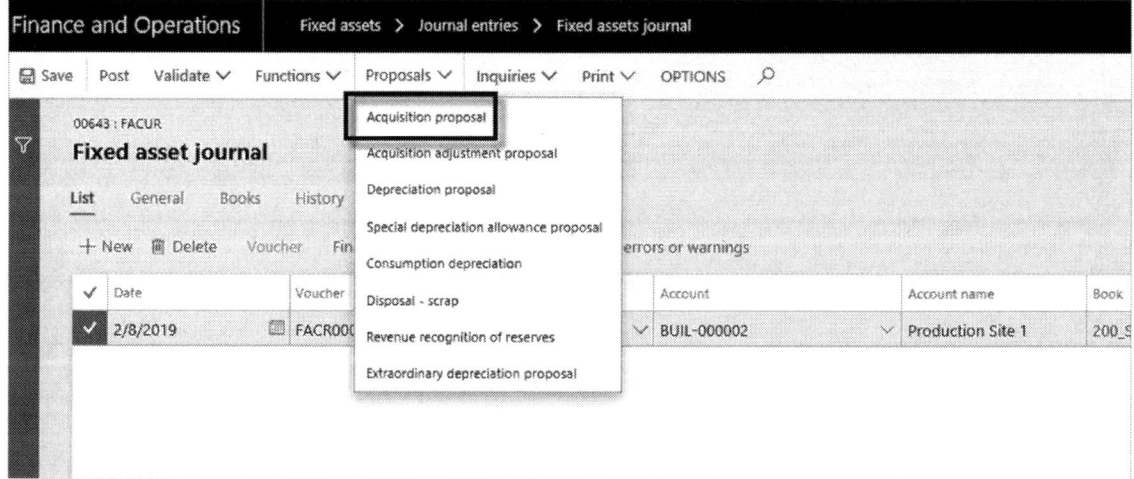

5. Line(s) are created
    1. Click Books tab (optional)

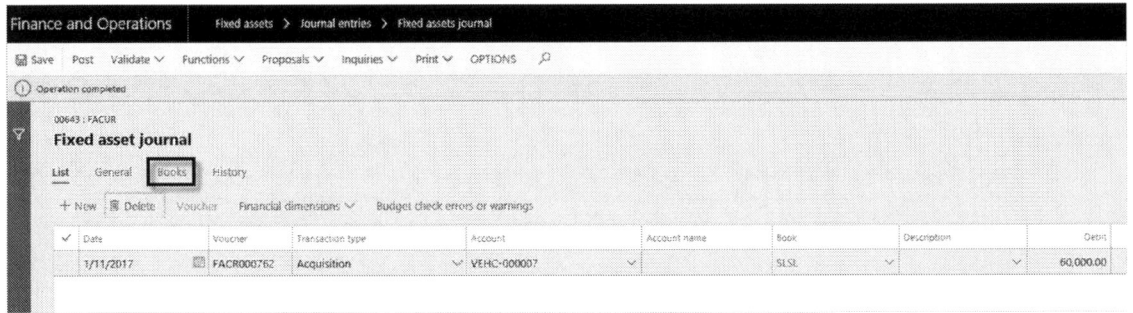

6. Post

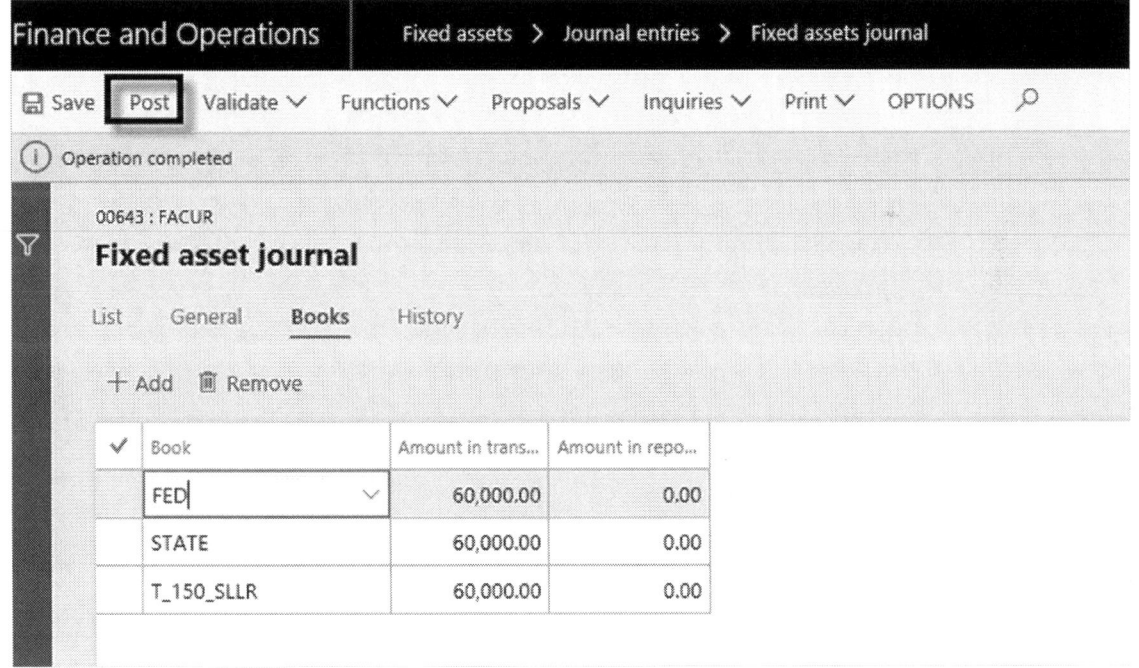

Fixed Asset Purchasing Parameters

Setup

1. From Fixed Assets open Fixed asset parameters
   1. Allow asset acquisition from Purchasing - Post a fixed asset when a vendor invoice is posted.
   2. Restrict asset acquisition posting to user group - Allow only members of the group to post fixed asset transactions.
   3. Create asset during product receipt or invoice posting - Create a new fixed asset when you post a product receipt, or when you post a vendor invoice if the fixed asset was not created when you posted the product receipt.
   4. Check for fixed assets creation during line entry - If selected, the fixed asset group is set on the purchase order line, according to the defined fixed asset rules, when the purchase order line is created.

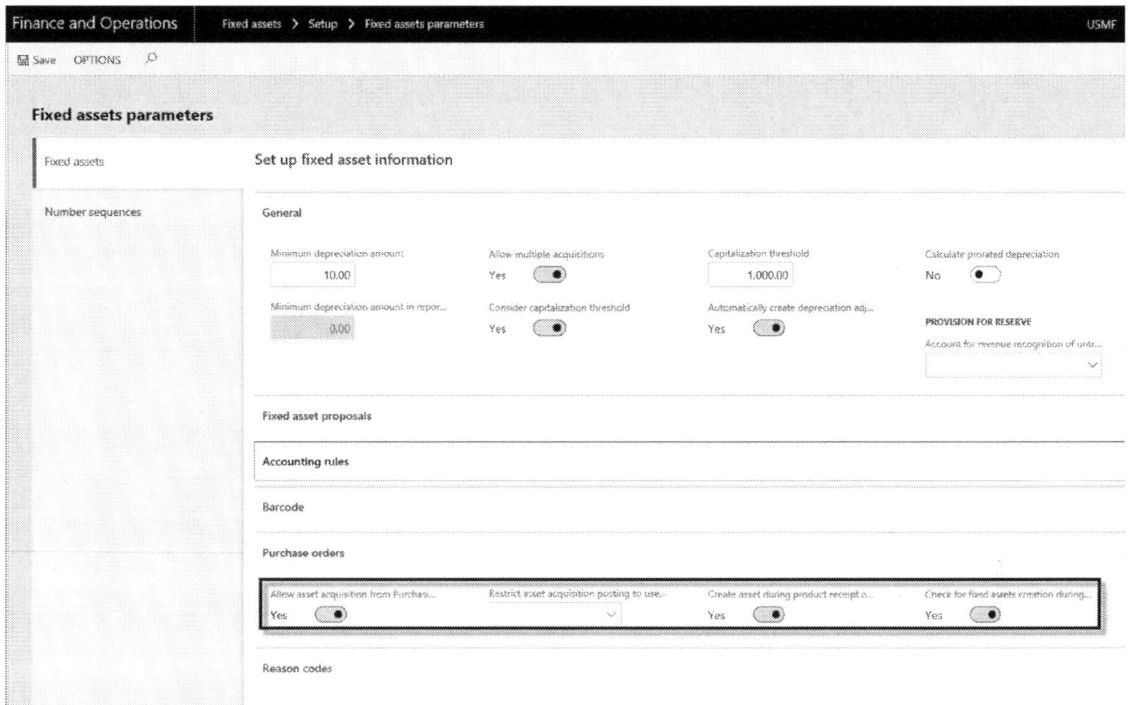

Fixed assets parameters

| Fixed assets |
| Number sequences |

Set up fixed asset information

General

| Minimum depreciation amount: | Allow multiple acquisitions | Capitalization threshold | Calculate prorated depreciation |
| 10.00 | Yes | 1,000.00 | No |

| Minimum depreciation amount in repor... | Consider capitalization threshold | Automatically create depreciation adj... | **PROVISION FOR RESERVE** |
| 0.00 | Yes | Yes | Account for revenue recognition of unre... |

Fixed asset proposals

Accounting rules

Barcode

Purchase orders

| Allow asset acquisition from Purchasi... | Restrict asset acquisition posting to use... | Create asset during product receipt p... | Check for fixed assets creation during... |
| Yes | | Yes | Yes |

Reason codes

Depreciation Profile

1.   From Fixed Assets open Depreciation Profiles

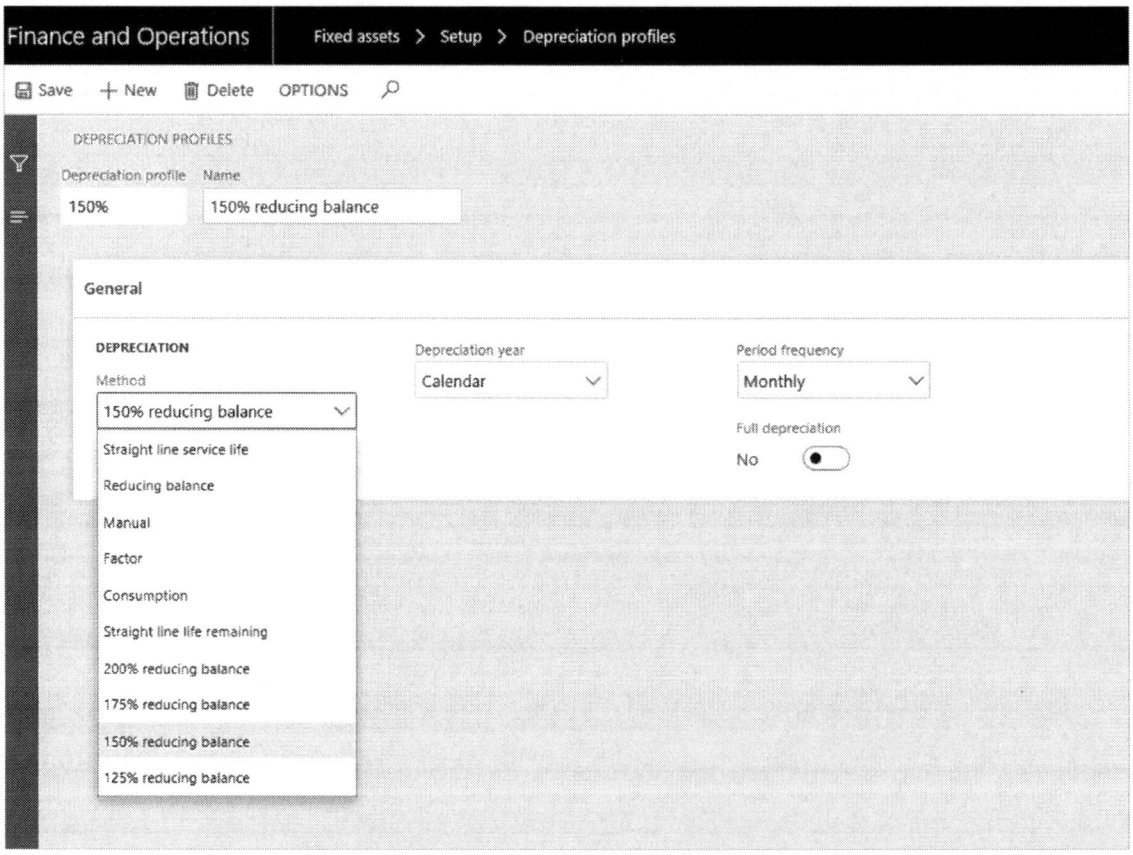

1. Note that method selections affect subsequent parameter displays
   1. Example, straight line service

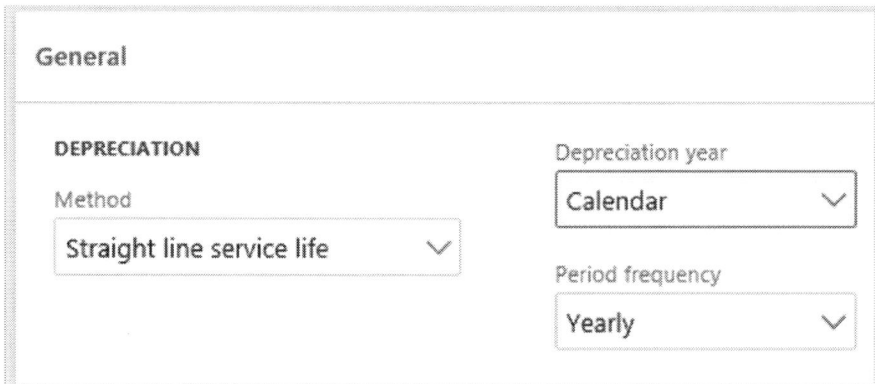

   2. Example, reducing balance

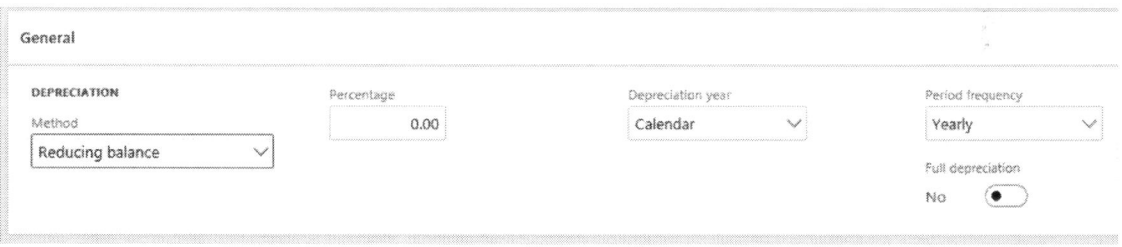

2. Depreciation Profiles are used with Depreciation Books

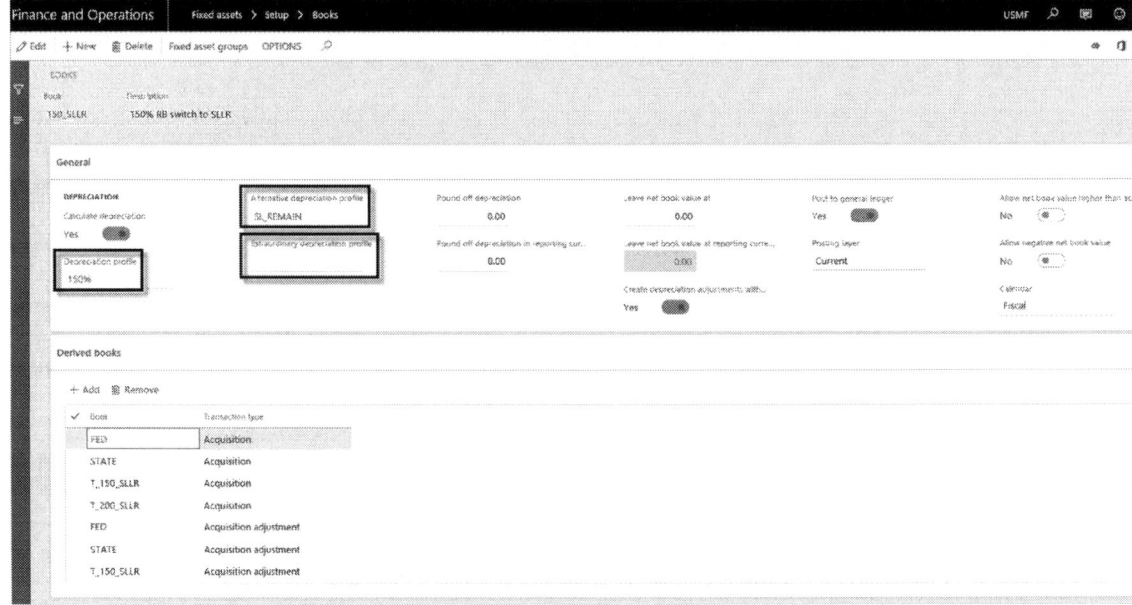

3.   Books attached to fixed assets are setup in a particular posting layer that is associated with a particular depreciation objective
         1.   As an example the Current layer is typically used for daily transactions and the Operations layer for fixed asset transactions
         2.   Note the layers used in Contoso for the fixed asset journal setups to verify this arrangement

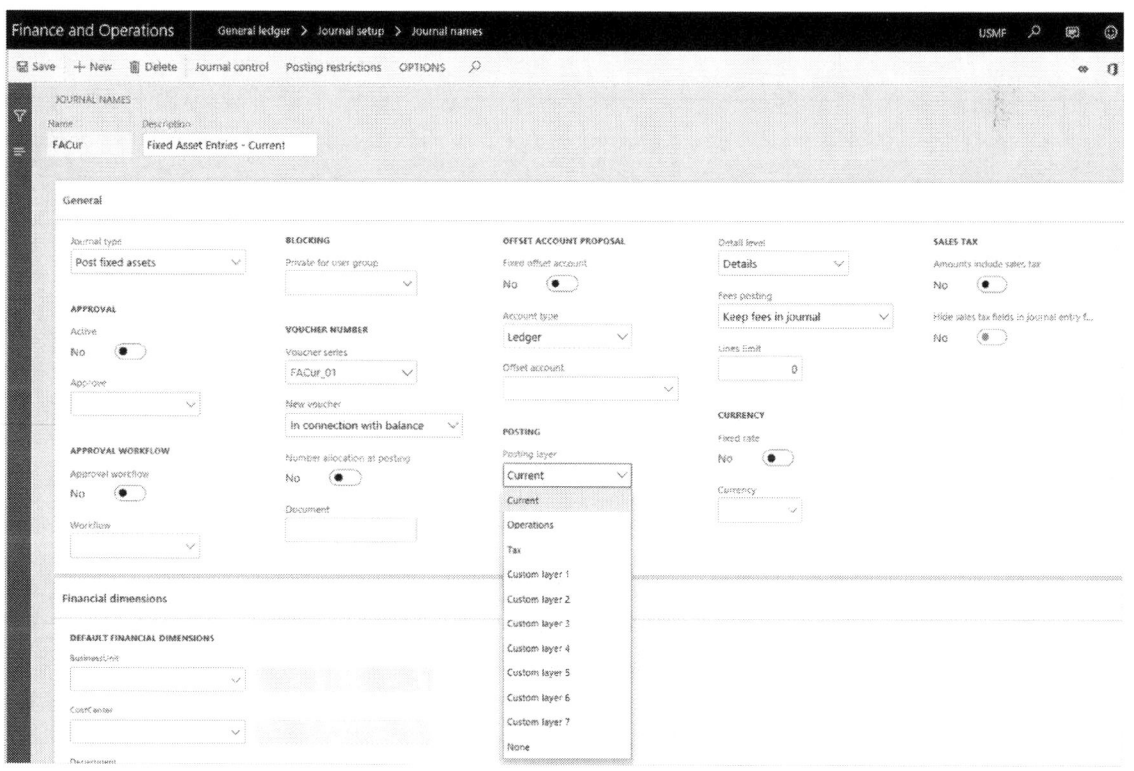

TAX

Sales Tax Codes

1. From Tax open Sales Tax Codes
   1. To edit value, click Sales tax code button

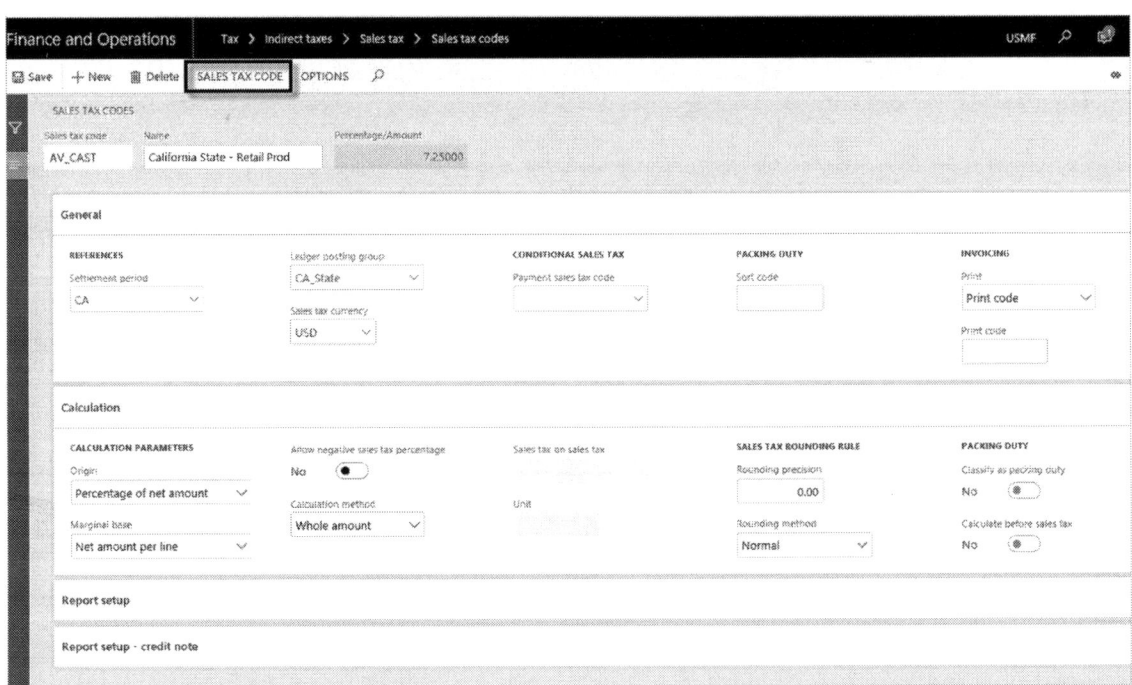

2. Update value field if required

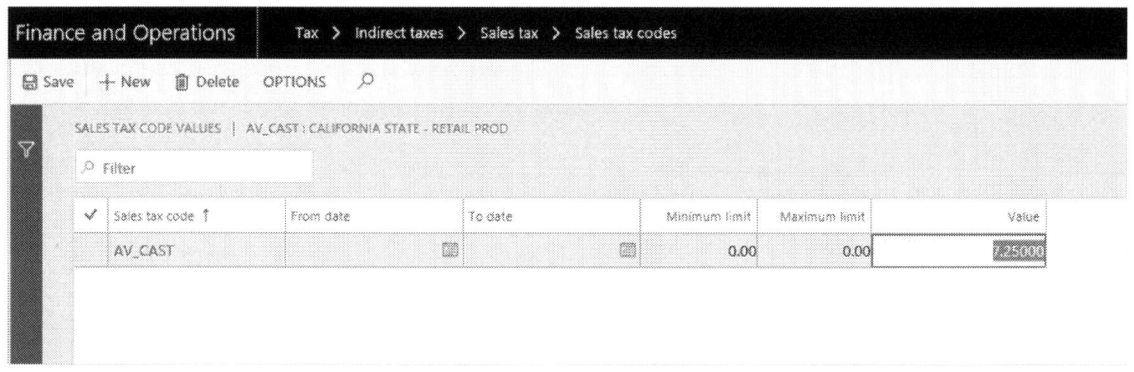

Sale Tax Settlement Periods and Codes

1. From Tax open Sales tax settlement periods

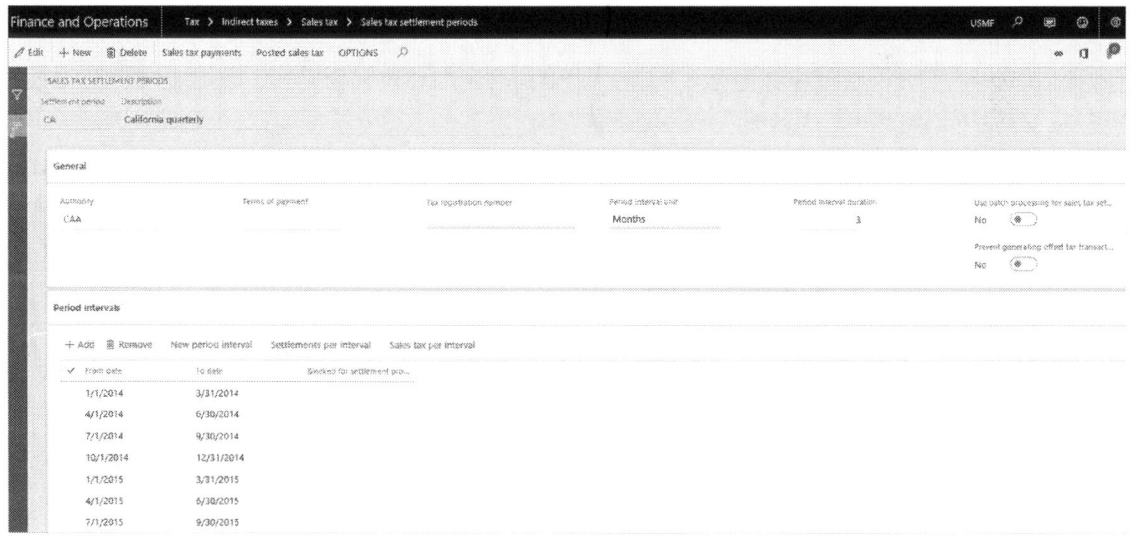

2.	Click New and input period parameters

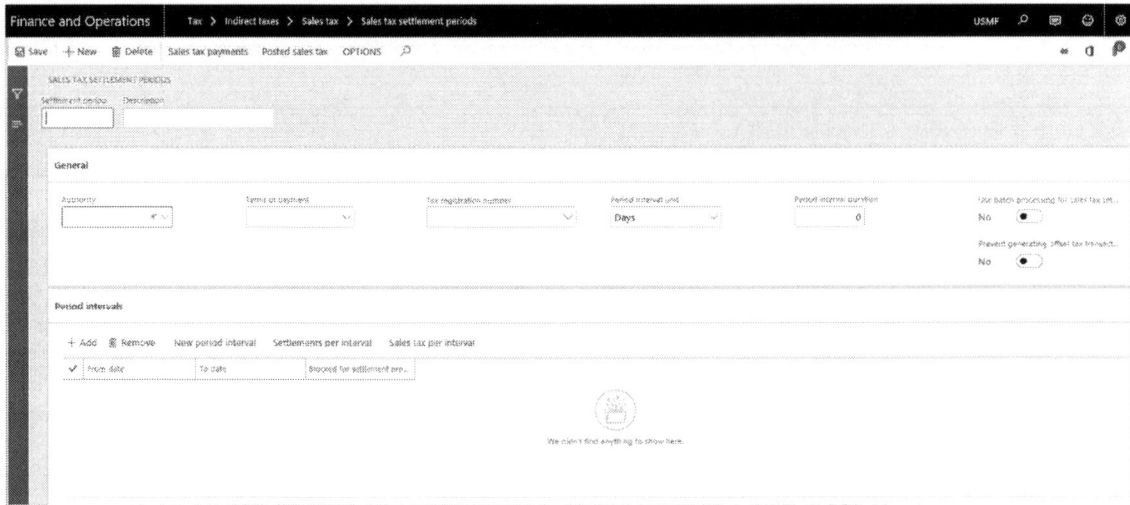

1.	Important note, if conditional sales tax is used, additional setups are required
2.	See MS docs: 'Setup conditional sales taxes' references; Sales taxes are usually reported in the period in which the invoice is created. However if a sales tax authority permits sales taxes and base amounts to be reported when the invoice is paid, use conditional sales taxes functionality. For invoices not fully settled with a single payment, sales taxes are reported and paid based on the amounts settled, not on the total amount of the invoice.
    1.	Important note, if tax authorities are <u>not set up as vendor</u>, automated payments cannot be used, and manual payments will need to be prepared.
    2.	Required by some countries: Create separate main accounts for sales taxes on invoices that are awaiting settlement, and create separate sales tax ledger posting groups to control the posting of conditional sales taxes to the separate main accounts.

3.   Create a separate settlement period for conditional sales taxes aligned with the settlement period for ordinary sales taxes, and for reporting to the sales tax authority.

4.   Create and align two sales tax codes: one for the conditional sales tax and one for the sales taxes that need to be reported.

1.   Note percentage amount which can also be updated via the Sales tax code button

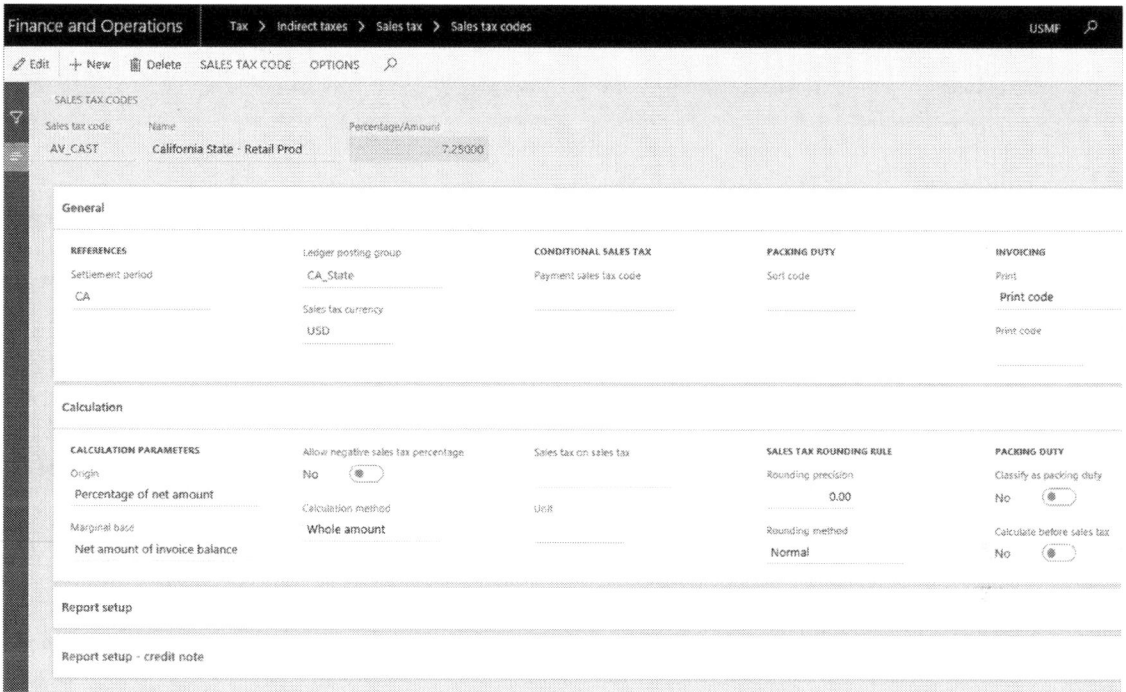

5.   Select the Conditional sales tax check box in the Sales tax area of the General ledger parameters form.

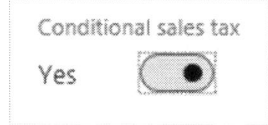

6. Every posted sales transaction must be set up for sales tax groups and item sales tax groups that contain one of the two created sales tax codes.

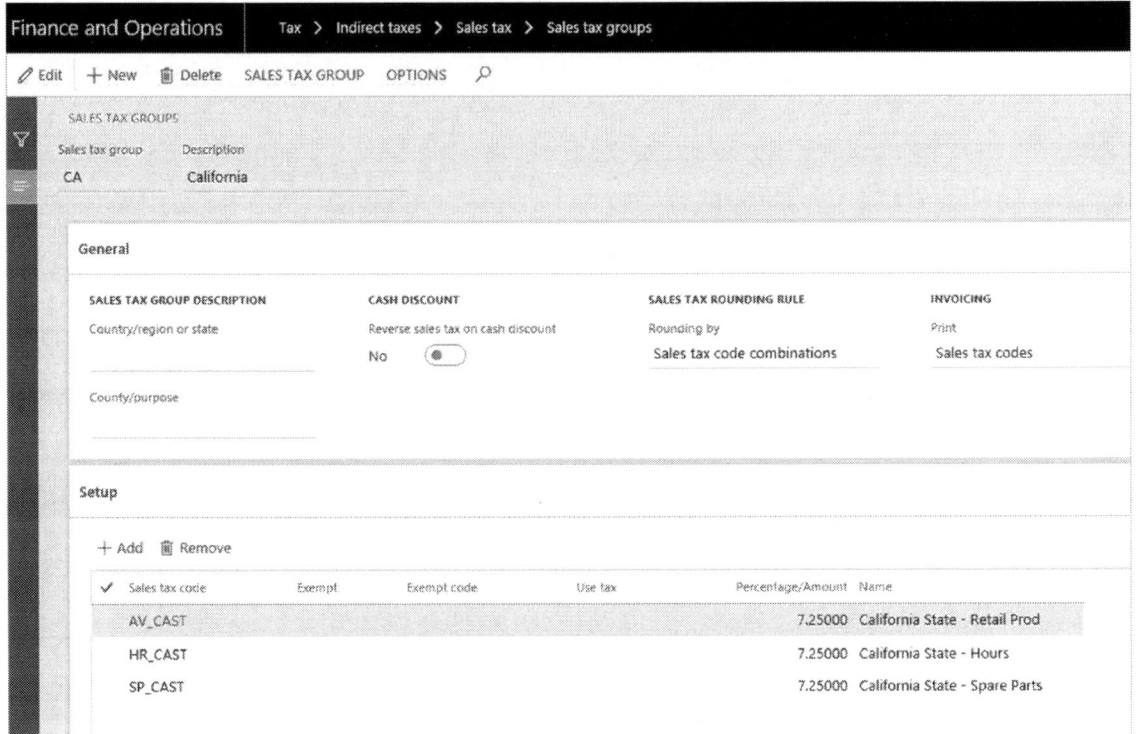

SO Sales Tax page

1.   From Accounts Receivable select a sales order
      1.   From the Sell action tab click Sales Tax
            1.   Also available from Lines

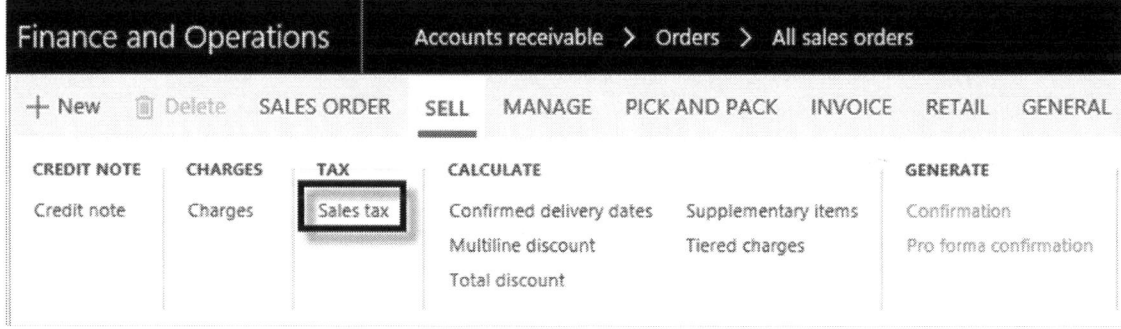

2. To revise, click Adjustment

Temporary sales tax transactions

Overview   General   Amount   **Adjustment**

Apply actual amounts   Reset actual from calculated amounts

✓	Sales tax code	Currency	Amount origin	Adjusted amou...	Calculated nond...	Actual nondedu...	Calculated sales...	Actual sales tax...	Override calcula...
	AV_CAST	USD	0.00	0.00	0.00	0.00	0.00	0.00	☐

Total calculated sales tax amount   Total actual sales tax amount

0.00   0.00

CASH and BANK MANAGEMENT

Bank Reconciliation

1. From Cash and Bank Management open Bank Accounts
   1. Typically done monthly
   2. (is related to the bridging accounts, see above)
   3. Click Reconcile and Account reconciliation

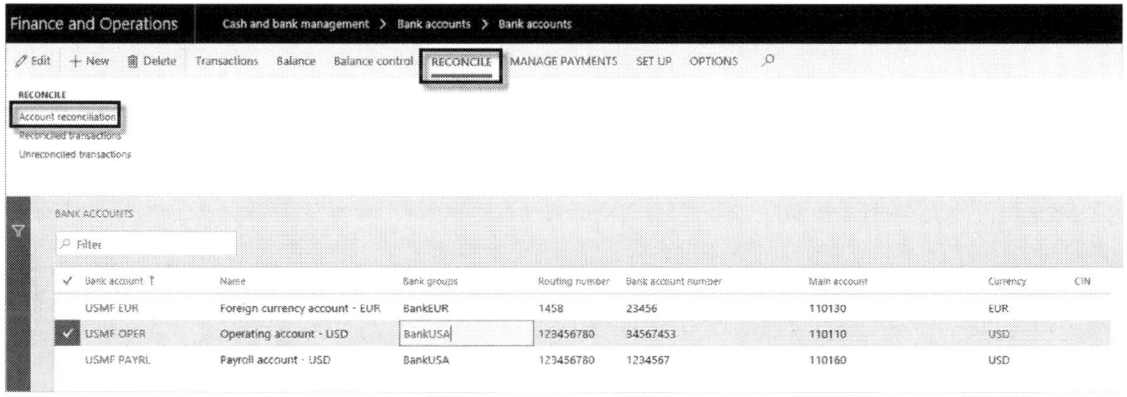

2. Click New, and enter date, number, and ending balance, and click Save
    1. Transactions button will enable, click Transactions

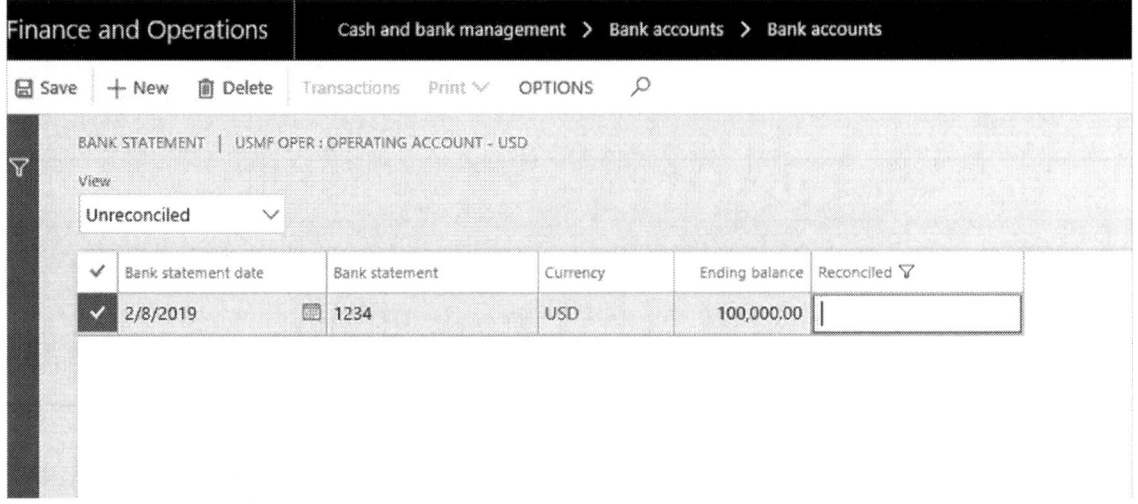

3. Mark transactions, click Save
    1. Continue transactions selection until the unreconciled field at <u>bottom of form</u> = 0
    2. Transactions can also be added or deleted
4. Click Reconcile accounts
    1. Button is enabled when amount = 0

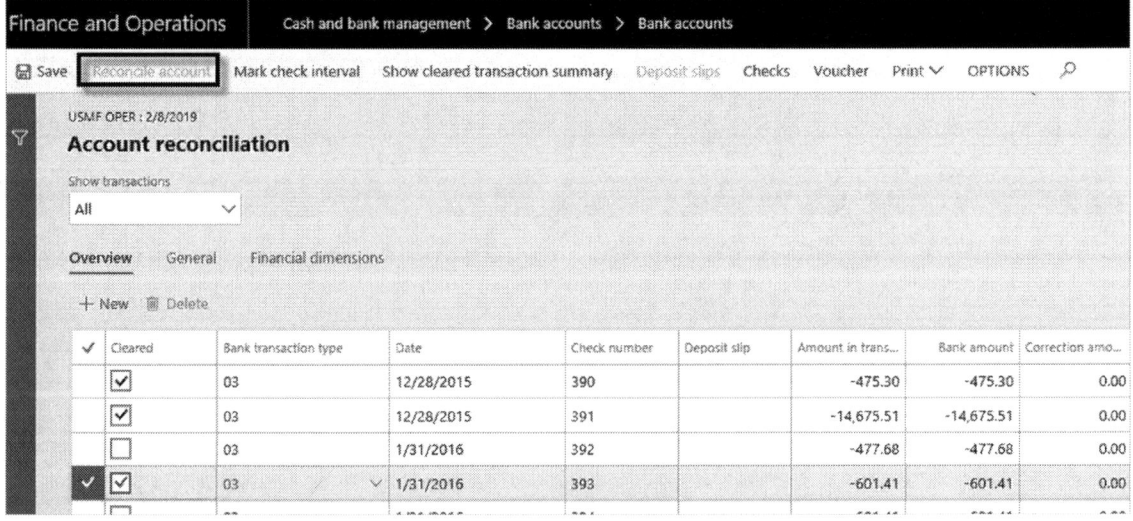

Wire Transfer Setup

1.   From Cash and Bank Management open Bank Transaction Groups
   1.   Create group
   2.   Create type

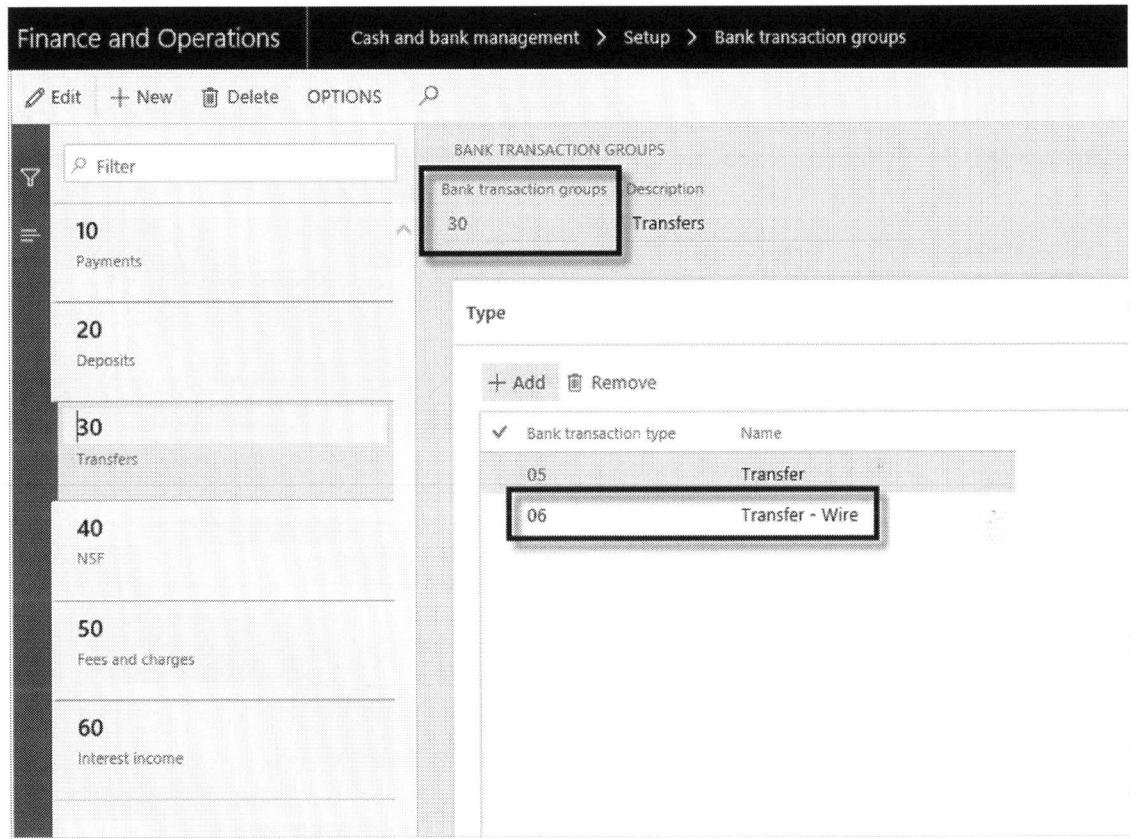

Check Layout

1.   From Cash and bank management open Bank Accounts

    1.   From the setup action tab click check

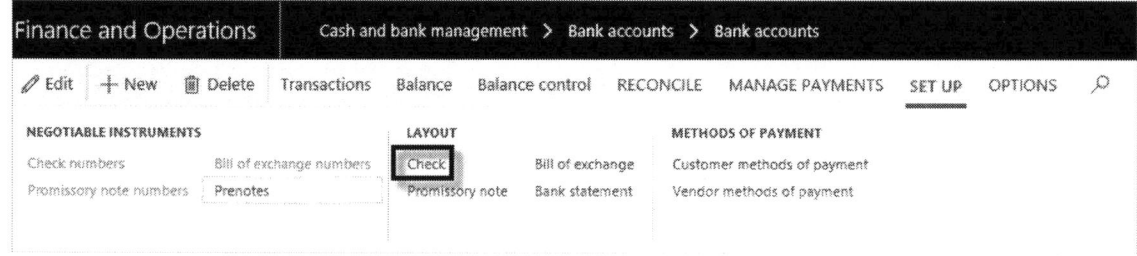

    2.   Apply format parameters

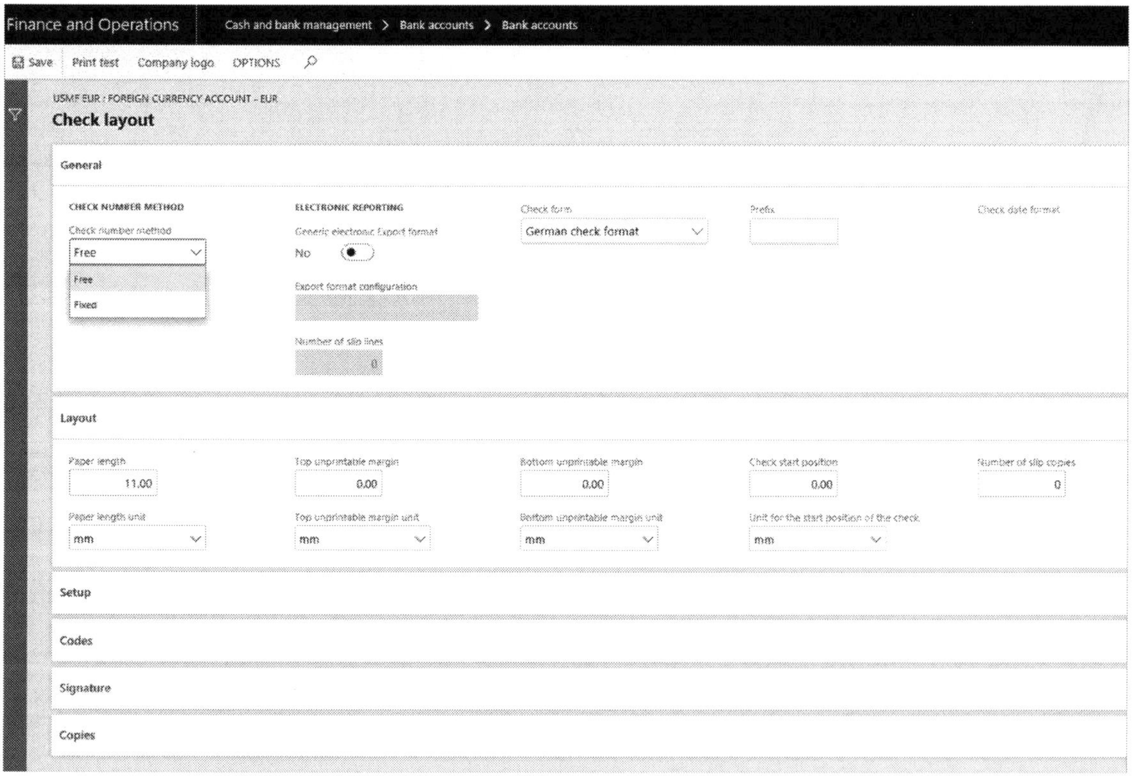

Bank Groups

1.   From Cash and Bank Management open Bank Groups
         1.   Bank Groups simplify Bank Account creation

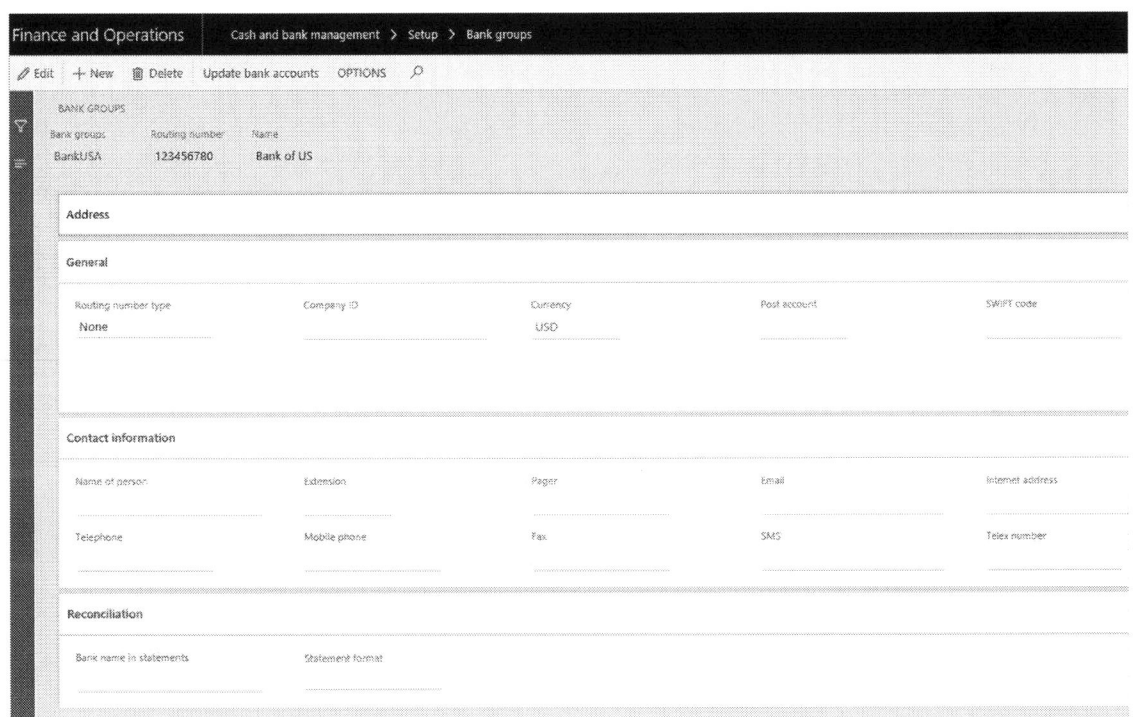

CREDIT and COLLECTIONS

Customer Collections Ageing

1.   From Credit and Collections open Aged Balances

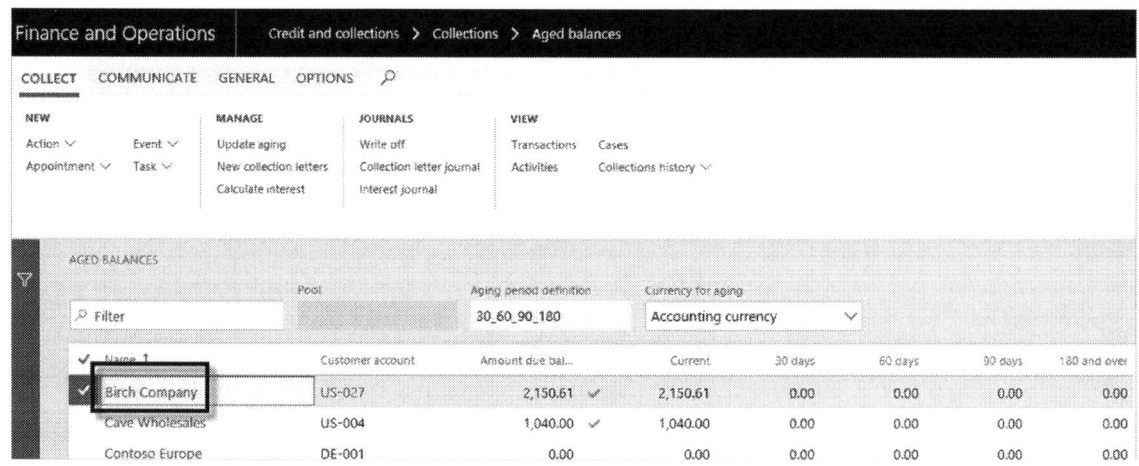

2. Click Customer name hyperlink (above) for transaction details

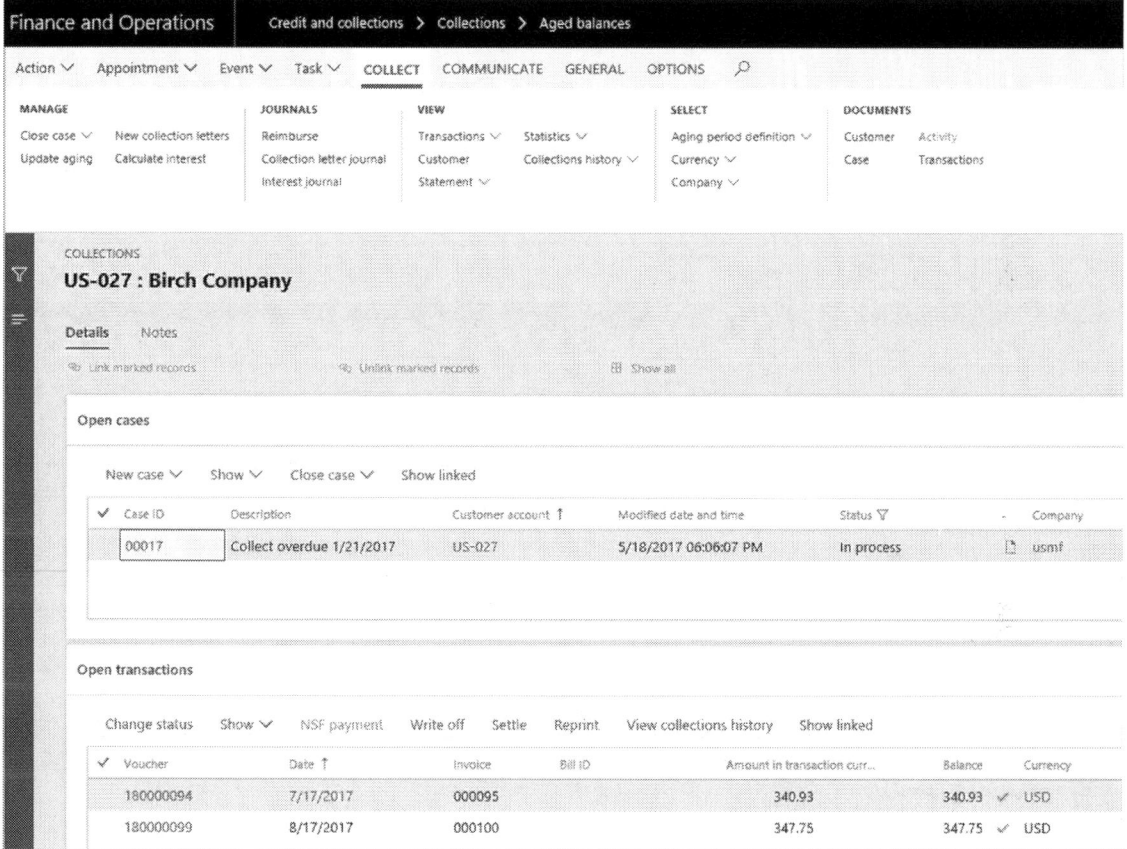

Customer Pools

1.   From Credit and Collections open Customer Pools
     1.   Defines customer account grouping that can be managed for collections
     2.   Use in conjunction with Customer agents and ageing snapshots
     3.   Click preview to view customer assignments

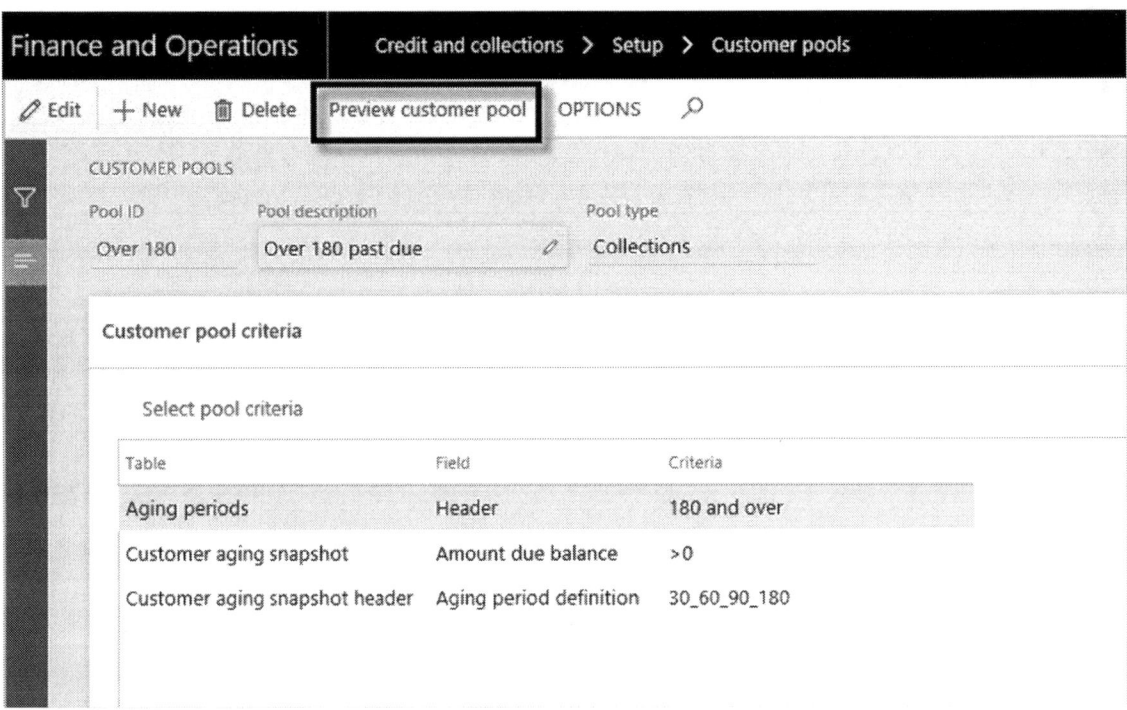

Credit Limit Configuration

1.   From <u>Accounts Receivable</u> open Accounts Receivable Parameters
   1.   On the Credit Rating fast tab select the Credit Limit Type Parameters. See MS docs: 'Credit limits for customers' references:
      1.   None – Do not check credit limits. You can override this option for a specific customer by selecting the Mandatory credit limit check box in the Customers form. If you do this, the credit limit is checked against the customer balance.
      2.   Balance – The credit limit is checked against the customer balance.
      3.   Balance + packing slip or product receipt – The credit limit is checked against the customer balance and deliveries.
      4.   Balance+All – The credit limit is checked against the customer balance, deliveries, and open orders.

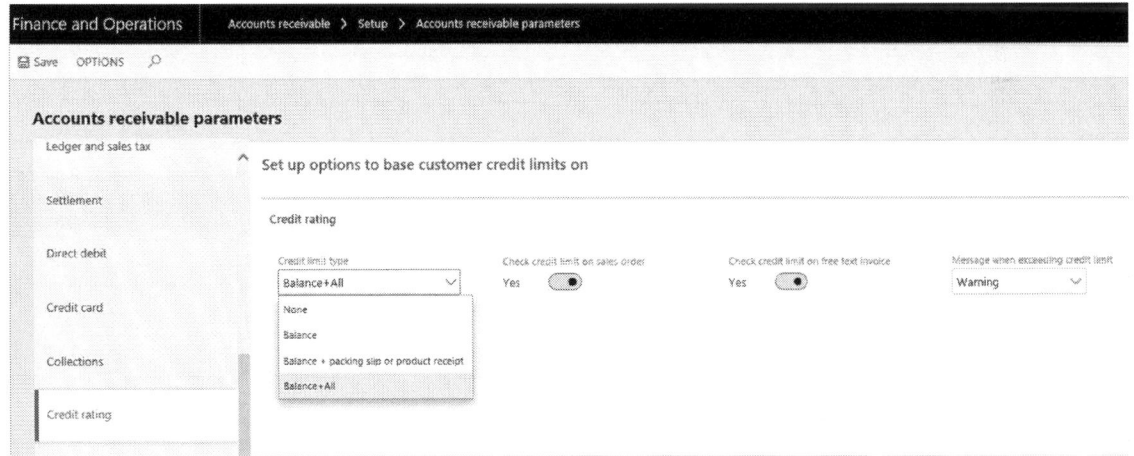

Collection Letters

1. From Credit and Collections open Customer posting profiles. (see MS docs 'Process collection letters')
   1. Collection letter sequence can be left blank

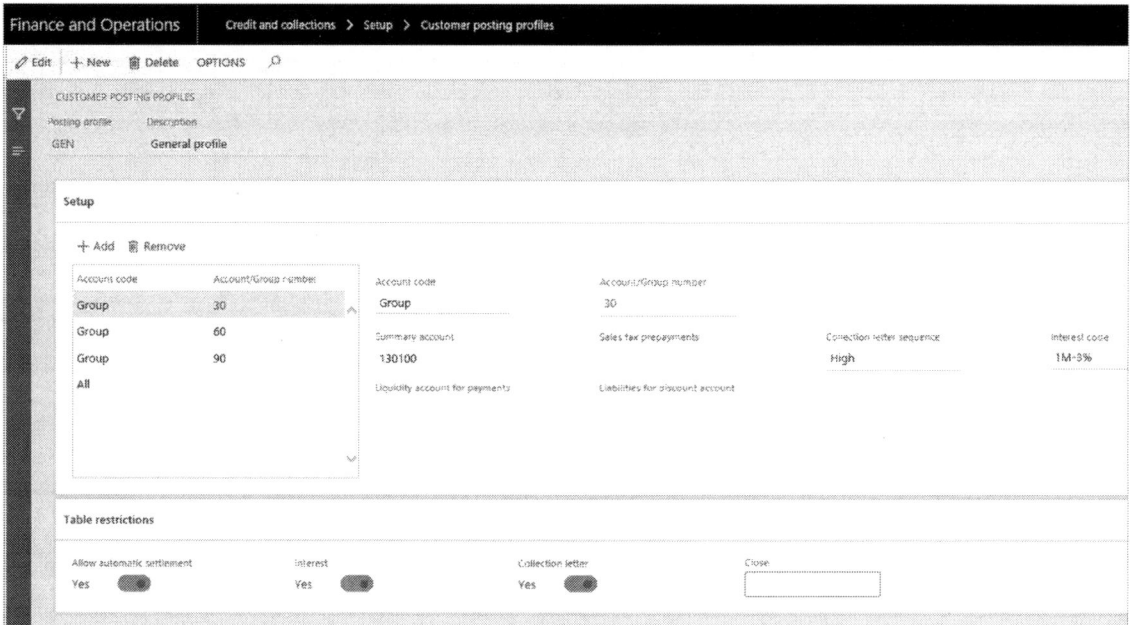

2.   Note Collection letter sequence

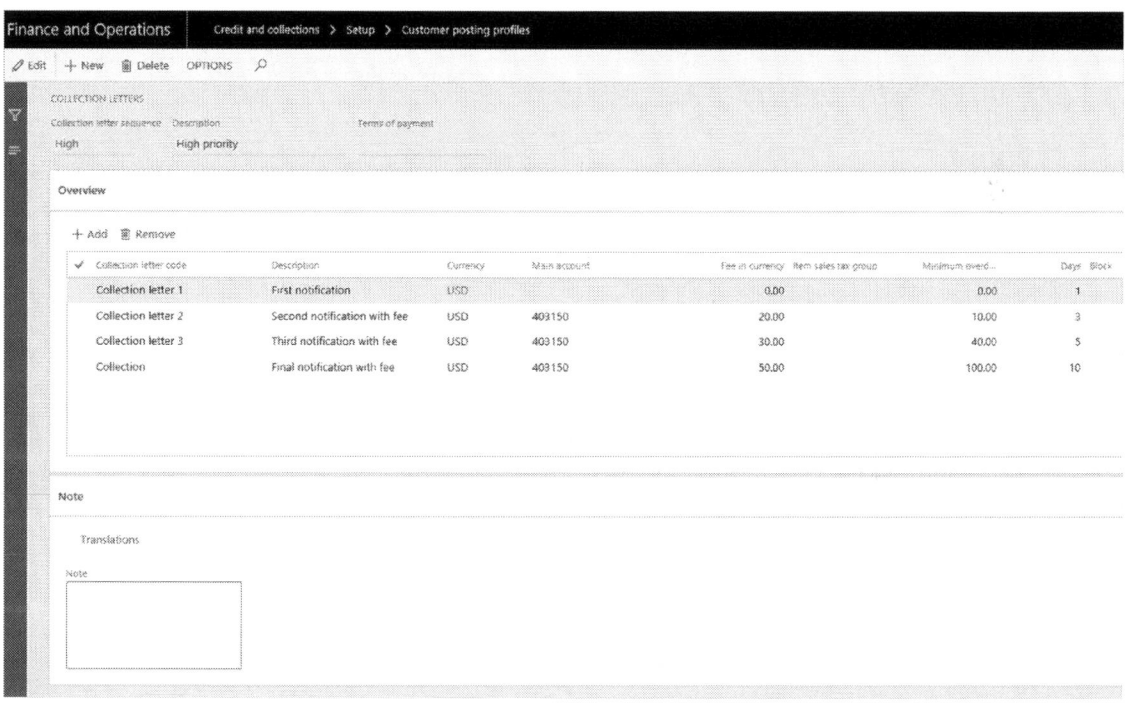

2.   Open Create collection letters

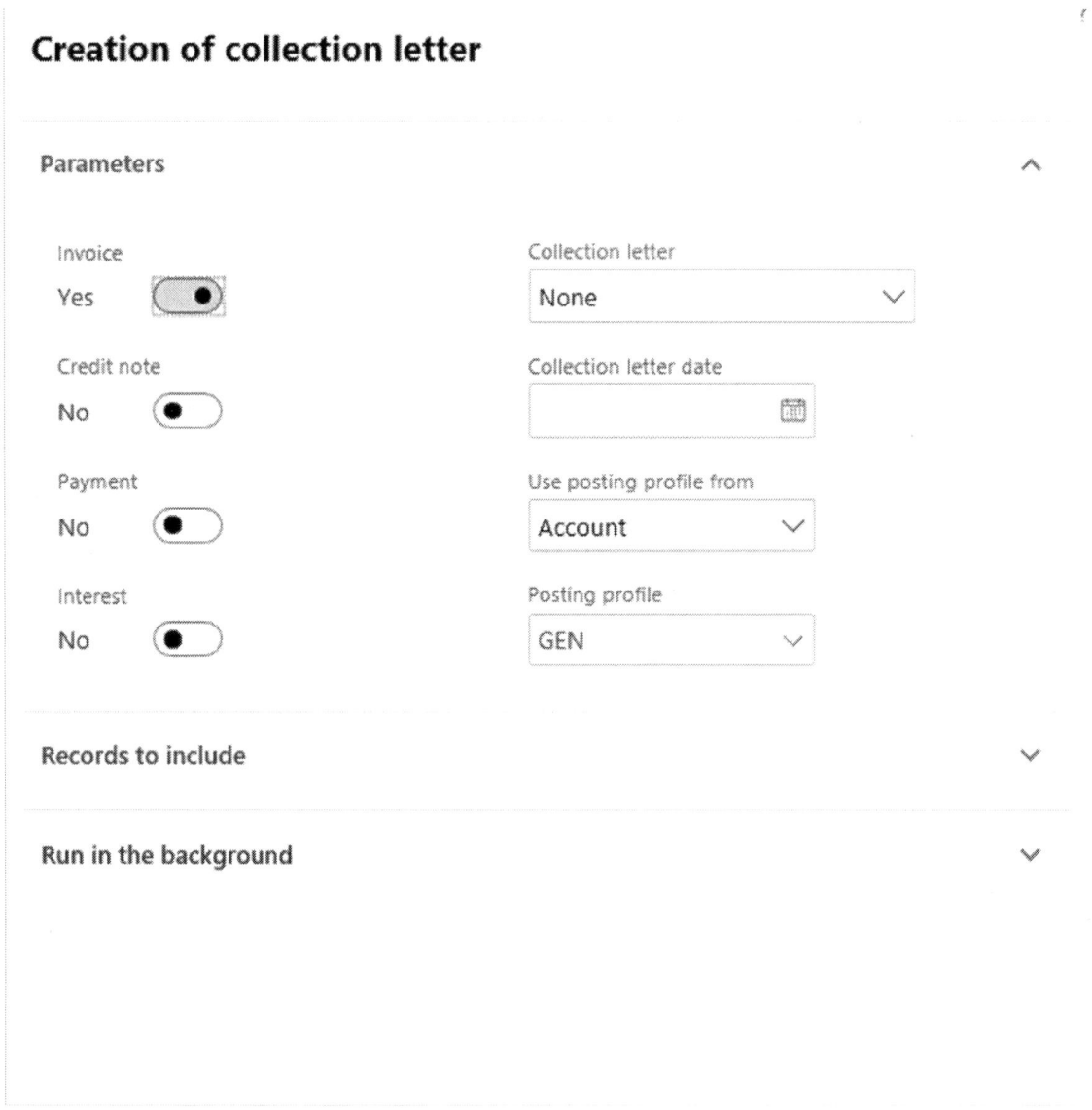

Creation of collection letter

Parameters   ⌃

Invoice   Collection letter
Yes   (●) | None   ⌄ |

Credit note   Collection letter date
No   (●) | 🗓 |

Payment   Use posting profile from
No   (●) | Account   ⌄ |

Interest   Posting profile
No   (●) | GEN   ⌄ |

Records to include   ⌄

Run in the background   ⌄

3. Open Review and process collection letters
    1. Status is
        1. Created
        2. Posted
        3. Cancelled

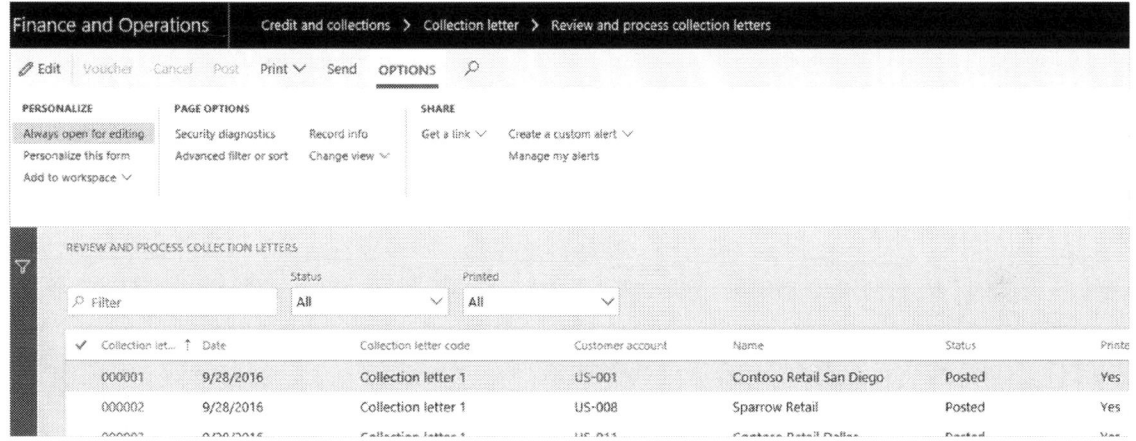

END

Good Luck!

NOTES

Printed in Great Britain
by Amazon

59603627R00071